Bill.

Happy special

much lov.

Jimmy.

RETURN TO INDIA

May 14th 1989.

Bill Bradly –
Bletchley. 1989.

RETURN TO INDIA

Kedar Nath

CASSELL

Cassell Publishers Ltd
Artillery House, Artillery Row
London SW1P 1RT

Copyright © Kedar Nath 1988

First published 1988

Distributed in the United States by
Sterling Publishing Co, Inc,
2 Park Avenue, New York, NY 10016

Distributed in Australia by
Capricorn Link (Australia) Pty Ltd
PO Box 665, Lane Cove, NSW 2066

British Library Cataloguing in Publication Data

Nath, Kedar
Return to India.
1. India – (Republic). Description & travel
I. Title
915.4'0452

ISBN 0–304–32220–2

Typeset by Inforum Ltd, Portsmouth
Printed and bound in Great Britain by
Biddles Ltd, Guildford and King's Lynn

Contents

Homecoming

Back home in Delhi after about ten years in Europe, I was confronted with some of the old problems again. Catching a bus during the rush-hour, for instance, struck me as a tricky affair. It called for agility and a 'me-first' attitude. This was particularly true when, as often happened, the vehicle halted anything between 50 and 100 metres from the stop. The queue would break up, and there followed a confused struggle to get on to the bus. Patient passengers always lost out.

I spoke about this to a friend, a columnist on a local paper.

'But it's a regular feature here,' he told me, citing the latest figures to show that the city needed twice as many buses as were currently being operated by the Delhi Transport Service. 'And what buses we're blessed with are always overcrowded,' he added. 'To crown it all, the bus driver tends to blame the public for it. He seems to enjoy humiliating them. The further he makes people run, the greater the kick he gets out of it.'

One afternoon, while sitting on a bus, I caught sight of this notice in English:

EVE-TEASING IS AN OFFENCE.
PUBLIC ARE REQUESTED TO CO-OPERATE.

Obviously the expression 'Eve-teasing' meant 'teasing the girls'. But was this popular pastime an offence? And were the public to co-operate in committing or in preventing the so-called offence? At best, the wording suggested unconscious humour. Then I happened to see the same notice in Hindi and was left in no doubt about the meaning: 'Molesting women is an offence; passengers are asked to kindly check it'. This, however, implied that women still needed legal protection on a public conveyance. I turned to the girl in the next seat. She wore jeans and was pretty in a tough-looking way, not the type one could hope to

7

'tease' with impunity. And I told myself that perhaps the notice had a different sort of woman in view.

I wanted to get off at the next stop, so I went to the back of the bus. Near me on the platform stood a couple in their early thirties, each carrying a baby. The traffic-lights had changed to red and the conductor asked them not to leave the bus. But the man, a stocky Sikh in a flame-coloured turban, jumped off, and the woman made a move to follow him out. Just then the bus lurched forward. The woman landed on the side of the road, with the child still in her arms. She stumbled, then steadied herself. At this some of the passengers made sounds and gestures of pity.

'Here in Delhi your family trembles for your safety,' said one of them, 'until you return home at the end of the day.'

'If you are careless,' said another, 'you are sure to get killed.'

A third man put in: 'If you are careful you run the risk of being run over; but if you are careless, it's all up with you.'

'For my part,' said a fourth man, 'I always carry in my pocket a card with my name and address whenever I leave home.'

Shortly afterwards I dropped into the post office in Connaught Place, New Delhi. I asked the counter clerk for two 2-rupee stamps. Briskly he handed them to me, together with 70 rupees change.

'But I gave you a 100-rupee note,' I told him.

A frown appeared on his thin clean-shaven face, followed by a nod; he passed me a 10-rupee note. Then, as if he had finished with me, he began serving another customer.

'What about the rest?' I asked.

In reply, he pressed his lips together.

I waited.

He was now attending to a third customer.

'Do you mind settling my business first?' I said. 'You still owe me 16 rupees.'

'I'm out of small change,' he retorted. 'I can only pay you when I get it from other customers.'

'How long will it take?' I asked. 'I've been standing here for nearly fifteen minutes.'

The man's dark face turned a pale grey.

'Let me have the stamps and the change I gave you,' he said.

Surprised by the sharp tone of his voice, I held them out and he snatched them out of my hand.

'Here!' And he flung my 100-rupee note back at me.

With a look of injured dignity he then turned to his colleague, who bore an uncanny resemblance to him. Above the noise and clatter of the post office they began speaking to each other, discussing my iniquity.

The Plaza Restaurant, where I had an appointment with a friend that afternoon, was within walking distance of the post office, next door to the Regal Cinema. We found a table by a large window overlooking the busy street. It was a smart and rather expensive sort of place. The table-cloth and napkins were spotless, but the seat springs had lost their elasticity. The waiter was so attentive that every few minutes we had to pick up the menu and order something.

Excusing myself for a minute, I went through the restaurant's crowded coffee bar, dimly lit like the inside of a cave, with its taped music blaring out. I emerged into a narrow passage and opened a door marked Gentlemen. Inside was a large room with a tiled floor and white walls, a couple of stalls to the right and a row of urinals to the left. A moustached man in khaki, about 30 and on the plump side, stood by the wash-basin near the entrance. He made a deep bow, giving me a broad smile.

Thinking he had mistaken me for someone else, I nodded and smiled back at him.

After a moment, I looked over my shoulder and saw that he had turned on the water tap. Impressed by this courtesy, I hurried over to the wash-basin, where he handed me a cake of soap. I now realized that he was the toilet attendant. Obviously he had not been going out of his way to be nice to me for purely humanitarian reasons.

Before I had even finished washing my hands, he passed me a towel. And hardly had I dried my fingers, when he offered me a comb. No, thank you, I told him. But he insisted that my hair could do with a bit of grooming, so I took out my own pocket comb.

Then he dropped to his knees before me and grabbed my right foot. I jumped back in surprise. 'Allow me, sir,' he said, reaching forward and wiping my shoes with a piece of cloth.

Next he looked at the tip I had given him. For a moment I thought he was going to fling it on the floor, but he controlled himself, turning away from me, without saying a word.

Back in the restaurant, I related the episode to my friend, a well-known satirist.

'This,' he remarked, 'is social evolution. Our values were once merely human; now they are merely commercial. Some people beg by stretching out their hands. But most people beg by forcing their services on you. They'll do anything to get money out of you. This fellow, for instance, would have masturbated you if he could have got paid for it. By the way, the man interests me. I'm going to pay him a short visit.'

Rejoining me after a while, he described what had taken place in the toilet. It was like a scene from a ballet. My friend was the first to bow and smile to the attendant; the first to run water in the wash-basin; using his handkerchief before being presented with a towel; and the first to whip out his comb. And then he thrust a paper napkin at the other to brush his shoes, saying that his own were already clean.

'Did you give him baksheesh?' I asked.

'I beat him at his own game, didn't I?' he grinned. 'So it was I who deserved a reward. Maybe he would even have tipped me, but he was simply dumbfounded.'

*   *   *

The voice answering the telephone sounded dry and rather impatient. It changed when I gave my name.

'Welcome back home, old boy!' exclaimed Dev.

We had not seen each other for ages; when I was last in India, some ten years previously, he had been abroad with Ulla, his Finnish wife.

'It's a pity your letter didn't say when you were arriving,' he now remarked. 'We're off to Kashmir in a couple of hours. Yes, we hope to do a bit of skiing. But we'll be back in two weeks – on January 5th to be exact.'

I told him we would get together on their return. He said Ulla wanted a word with me and she greeted me in her rather high-pitched voice.

'And how is Europe?' she asked.

I gave a suitable answer.

'India has made enormous progress,' she suddenly declared. 'It has become greater than ever.'

About three weeks later, Dev rang me up. Could I give them the pleasure of my company the following day? I said I was at their disposal. He had to plead a case in the High Court but would be free in the afternoon. He would pick me up in Connaught Place on his way home.

The sky was overcast; a cold wind had sprung up. The arcade in which I stood at the agreed spot bustled with activity. Along its open side was a sprinkling of betel and cigarette stands, and some vendors had set out on the floor their displays of fancy jewellery, hand-painted screens and other articles to draw in tourists. I was watching the traffic and suddenly became aware of someone standing next to me. I turned and saw a barefoot, plainly dressed young woman with a pale roundish face.

She was holding a reed out to me, with about a dozen multicoloured balloons tied to it. They seemed to contain grains of corn, and rattled when she shook them. The price she asked was modest.

'What makes them worth so much?' I said.

She listed her expenses.

'And pumping air into balloons with the mouth often bring on headaches,' she added.

Then I noticed a black Jaguar pull into the kerb. A thin man stepped out, hurried over to the other side of the car and opened the door. Dev emerged from it, his dark suit showing off his tall athletic figure to perfection. We shook hands, exchanging greetings and compliments. As we got in, the thin man, obviously his assistant, shut the door behind us and took his seat next to the chauffeur, who moved into the line of traffic.

Dev threw an amused smile at the balloons.

'Where did you get these?' he asked.

I told him.

'Do you still play with such things?' he wanted to know.

'I bought them without thinking,' I said. 'Maybe it was because the woman had a little child on her arm and a bare-footed older one standing beside her.'

'Great!' he said with a somewhat theatrical laugh. 'Hoping to change the world by acts of private charity, eh? But these balloons are bound to be unhygienic. I never buy anything except from a proper shop. If you don't mind, I'll get rid of them for you.'

Then he asked his assistant in the front seat to take the balloons from me and told him how to dispose of them.

For a while we talked about old friends. Dev and I used to teach at the same college in North India about twenty years ago. Thanks to a modest inheritance, he soon left for England to study law. When I saw him in London a couple of years later, he was working at night as a booking-clerk for British Rail to help pay his way. He had just got married to an au pair girl from Helsinki: they met at a dance and it was a case of love at first sight. He took me to his flat – a cheerless room with a tiny kitchen. It was winter. The only source of warmth in the place was a small electric heater, and Ulla, his bride, seemed to shiver in her thin dress.

Things had changed since. Dev was now one of the top barristers in the capital and often argued cases in the Supreme Court. The year before he had made a trip to the United States to open an office in Washington in partnership with an Indian lawyer there; the practice was beginning to make money. He counted several foreign embassies in New Delhi among his clients. His only son, who attended a public school in England, was making splendid progress. Suddenly he drew my attention to the lush green of the boulevard we were driving along.

'Is Paris more beautiful than this?' he said. 'Is there a lovelier city in the world?'

We turned into South Extension, a residential district with an air of wealth and luxury about it. The car came to a stop in front of a yellow two-storeyed house in the middle of a large garden. The assistant went ahead of us to open the gate, carrying Dev's brief-case and my balloons. Two large Alsatian dogs came rushing from inside the house. Behind them appeared the gardener, a dark stocky man with a hoe; the way the dogs obeyed his commands suggested that he was in charge of them too.

He gratefully received the balloons from the assistant. Dev played with the dogs for a minute, then showed me over the garden. He told me about one of his ambitions. On special occasions in earlier times, a ruler used to weigh himself against gold, diamonds or other precious stones. Then these were distributed among his subjects, adding to his fame and power. Nowadays, big public figures went in for that sort of thing. Dev named an industrialist, the head of a religious sect and a political leader, who had used bank notes to counterbalance their weight.

Though he could not afford such a ceremony yet, Dev hoped one day to have himself weighed against silver. He would then be a kind of national hero and making money hand over fist.

On a long table in the high-ceilinged living-room stood bottles of cognac, vodka, whisky and wine – imported drinks, generally unavailable. I remarked that they must have cost a fortune.

Dev grinned, saying: 'Nothing is too expensive for my friends.'

The cow is sacred to the Hindus, and pork is forbidden to the Muslims; yet there before me was a variety of dishes containing beef and pork. Asked how he got hold of such illicit ingredients, he answered with a mysterious air: 'Connections.'

His wife, looking rosy and plump, wore an exquisite sari. I made a complimentary remark about the furniture in the room. It was Finnish, she said.

Dev added: 'None can beat the Finns in quality and design.'

I looked at a modernistic painting on the wall, asking what it was supposed to be about.

'To tell the truth,' he said, 'I myself don't know. But the artist is said to be the Indian Picasso. It cost me a lot. But a man in my position has to keep up with the times.'

I asked Ulla how she spent her time. She said she led a busy life, being an active member of a couple of clubs. They did a lot of entertaining, too. What people did they generally invite? Oh, they had their circle of friends. The Finnish ambassador, for example, was one of their frequent guests.

She wanted to know whether I thought India had achieved great prosperity since my previous trip. I agreed that this was certainly true of the upper-middle class. I then related a scene I had witnessed.

A few days earlier, an acquaintance had taken me to a restaurant in an overcrowded street near the Jama Masjid mosque in old Delhi. There were always a great many beggars hanging around the place, and an almost equal number of dogs, too. After eating their fill, some of the customers ordered extra loaves of bread, which they threw to the beggars. I saw one beggar catch a loaf. Suddenly a dog next to him jumped up and snatched half of it out of his hand.

'It made me smile,' I said. 'And it brought a tear to my eye.'

Dev was evidently not impressed by my story.

'I've seen worse sights in the East End of London,' he maintained, dismissing the subject.

I asked when he had last visited old Delhi. Oh, maybe ten years ago. He had no time to waste; in fact, he never went there.

I told him I had made a sentimental trip to a part of old Delhi where I used to live as a student. It had become more congested than I remembered and the prostitutes' quarter of the old days was now a shopping centre.

'Yes, we've cleaned up the town,' Dev remarked rather pompously. 'But let's change the subject. Ulla isn't interested in the sordid aspects of life. Why can't we talk of nice things?'

At this point Ulla asked whether I had ever been to Udaipur, in Rajasthan state. She praised this 'city of sunrise', famous for its marble palaces of the seventeenth and eighteenth centuries, towering over the two islands on Lake Pichola.

I said I was thinking of going there.

'Then you positively must see the museum,' she suggested. 'It's so fantastic; there isn't another like it in the world. I've been to Jaipur many times,' she began, speaking of the capital of Rajasthan. 'Quite rightly is it called the pink city because it has a pink city wall with seven gateways and most of the buildings are pink, too.

'And the layout of Jaipur,' she went on, 'is matchless – the main streets are no less than 36 metres wide. The city palace, with its Hall of Winds and the Observatory, is a wonder of architecture. When you think all that dates from the eighteenth century! To my mind Jaipur is the most beautiful of cities,' she concluded.

Then I mentioned a problem. I was unable to send off some picture postcards I had bought because only postage stamps of low value were available: you had to use so many that there was no space left for the address.

Dev refused to believe it, saying that I could have stamps of any value from the main post office in Parliament Street. I did not tell him that I had been there. Instead, I remarked that no money-order forms could be had at any post office, according to my local postmaster.

'The postmaster,' retorted Dev, 'was lying. There are people who lie for the sake of lying.'

As he was seeing me off, I asked:

'Has Ulla ever been to the slums of old Delhi?'

He looked at me as if I were mad.

'Why should she?' he said. 'One has to create one's own environments, you know.'

The Telegram

The telephone rang one morning. On the line was Fikr Taunsvi, the writer.

'I've almost finished my piece for tomorrow's edition,' he told me. For twenty-five years he had been writing a daily satirical column, entitled Onionskins, for the *Milap*, India's leading Urdu-language newspaper. 'I'll be free around one o'clock. How about lunch together?'

'I've a special reason for wanting to see you,' I said. 'You mentioned that a book of yours had been translated into Malayalam.'

'And you've got your eye on the royalties, eh?'

'I won't deny that. But you must know a lot about Kerala.'

'Just because my book is coming out in the Malayalam language? I've never been to South India.'

'Me neither. But I'm going there now.'

'What has inspired you?'

'A telegram from a friend in Kerala, asking me to come right away to that green wonderland of his. He himself is entering hospital for an operation, but his friends will look after me.'

'It's an opportunity you shouldn't miss. When do you plan to leave?'

'As soon as I get a booking. You have connections. Can you help me?'

'My son knows someone at the airline office who might fix you up.'

'I'd rather go by train, and second class – no first-class or air-conditioned luxury coach for me. It's more interesting that way: one meets people, gathers impressions. Don't you agree?'

We met in a restaurant in Connaught Place. Over lunch Fikr said:

'Shortly after our telephone conversation this morning, I discovered a curious little fact. Have you any idea when the first book was printed in India?'

'No,' I answered. 'When was it?'

'In 1577. And you know where? The port city of Cochin.'

'But that's in Kerala!'

'Exactly.'

'Is that why Kerala has the highest literacy rate among the states of India and why its women are said to be so high in the social scale?'

Fikr gave the amused smile I had expected.

'The book in question,' he said, 'was published by a religious order, called the Society of Jesus. And the exalted status of the women may partly be due to a historical reason – the matrilineal family system that has existed in Kerala for centuries. But now tell me about this friend who has invited you there.'

'He is called Varghese and he belongs to one of the world's oldest Christian sects, the Syrian Christians. They say it was founded by St Thomas, the Apostle, when he came to Kerala in the first century AD.'

'So he's carrying the weight of two thousand years of history on his back. What else does he do?'

'At present he is with an institute engaged in regional development studies at Kottayam.'

'And before that?'

'I got to know him in London. He was a market-research man for a cosmetics firm there. Materially he was doing quite well. But he was unhappy, dissatisfied with himself. He had all along felt that he should work for the welfare of his native Kerala. He maintained that making a career for himself in an affluent country was selfish and downright immoral.'

'How come that he was sticking it out there?'

'Love – he'd married an English girl in Delhi.'

'What was he doing then?'

'He'd been a brilliant student who won an American scholarship, taking a first-class degree in economics from the University of Kansas. For a while he was a college lecturer in Bombay and Madras. Then he went into journalism. Before his departure for England, he was joint editor of a magazine called the *Social Scientist*.'

'Ah, a case of an intellectual haunted by his deserted ideals.'

'That's just what it was. I last saw him the day his divorce came through. He'd given up his market-research job and was returning to India the same weekend.'

'How much time has passed since?'

'Oh, nearly eleven years. I lost his address; he didn't have mine, as I'd left Britain for the continent. I got wind of his whereabouts only two weeks ago.'

'OK,' said Fikr. 'The railway booking office is close by. Let's see about your journey.'

We left the restaurant. After a few minutes we stopped in front of a large single-storeyed building. On its right, anchored to a mast, was a

loudspeaker, blaring out popular music that followed us all the way into the booking-hall. The whole place echoed with the noise.

'Who is this earache meant for?' asked Fikr.

'For VIPs like you and me,' I answered.

'The chief of the booking office must be in partnership with an ear doctor,' he said.

The space in front of the ticket windows was packed with people. I went to one where the crowd appeared smaller. The booking-clerk was a slim young woman in a necklace of imitation pearls. She was staring hard at a fat man who was protesting that she had not answered his enquiry properly. Her right hand made a sudden movement, catching up the lower end of her necklace.

'Stop it,' she shouted at the man. 'You've had the necessary information. Please make room for the others now.'

'She's bad-tempered,' remarked someone near me.

'So are all of them in this place,' said his neighbour.

Edging myself to the window, I greeted the booking-clerk. In reply she threw me a questioning look. I stated my business. She asked me to check the reservation plan, which was arranged in a tabular form outside the window, with different-coloured pieces of plastic. I ran my eye over them. Not a single seat was free. I told the woman.

'Do you want to be put on the waiting-list?' she asked.

'I should prefer something definite.'

'Do you want to reserve a seat for the fourteenth?'

'But that's two weeks away!'

'I can't give you an earlier booking.' She glanced at her watch. 'We're closed for an hour.' And she disappeared.

Fikr suggested trying the reservation supervisor. A door beyond the ticket windows opened on to the main office, where clerks bustled about in the big room. It took several minutes to find the reservation supervisor, a tall thin man who cleared his throat at the beginning of each sentence. He asked why he should make an exception in my case. I replied that I had to visit someone in Kerala who was having a major operation. The official's steely blue eyes rested on me:

'Is this person a member of your family or a close relative of yours?'

'No, an old friend.'

'What is your occupation?'

I told him.

'What proof can you give me of his medical condition?'

'A letter and a telegram, but I haven't got them on me.'

'Why is your presence there so urgent?'

'Because I live abroad and am leaving India in a relatively short time.'

'You are neither a relative nor a surgeon. I can't help you.' Turning away, he added: 'Sorry.'

As we came out of the booking office, Fikr mentioned Bhullar. Bhullar, Dev and I had once been fellow lecturers at a college, where Bhullar had taught Indian history. For years this man had been telling people that he was leaving the civil service for a career as a writer. He published occasional pieces in India's English-language press, and he always sent everyone he knew a copy of the paper containing his contribution.

Recently he had asked me to his office at the Archaeological Survey of India. 'Imagine meeting after fifteen years!' he exclaimed when he saw me. He had gone bald on top, and the hair at his temples was dyed a purplish black, as was the stubble of his shaved eyebrows. He was very pleasant and shared with me the lunch he had brought from home. He told me about his literary bomb, a book he had 'practically finished'.

I now phoned him from a call box:

'Fikr tells me that some train seats are kept in reserve for ministry people or MPs. Is that right?'

When he confirmed it, I told him about my problem. 'You think you could help me? After all, you are an under-secretary.'

He promised to let me know the following day.

He did nothing of the sort, however.

So I rang him up again.

'I didn't call you because the Railway Minister didn't come to work,' he explained. It was shortly after elections and the opposition party had formed the Government. 'These ministers are new to their jobs and aren't punctual in their duties yet,' he added. 'The Railway Minister has always five seats at his disposal; he generally distributes them among his secretaries and typists for their relatives. The only promise I can make is that I'll try next Monday or Tuesday if the Minister turns up. But I can't hold out much hope. Perhaps you should cancel the Kerala trip and go somewhere else instead – to the Punjab, for instance.'

I thanked him and hung up. A moment later Dev was on the phone. I mentioned to him what Bhullar had told me.

'Bhullar is lying,' he said. 'The Railway Minister has nothing to do with seats or tickets, but with policy matters. I'll give you a tip.'

Following his advice, I made a bee-line for Baroda House, formerly the residence of the Maharaja of Baroda. There I walked into one of the offices.

'Is this where Indians resident abroad can book train seats?' I asked.

The clerk, an overweight friendly man with a bushy beard, nodded. He took a brief look at my passport.

'Do you want to leave tomorrow?' he enquired.

I did.

He gave me a form to fill out. In five minutes I had the authority. I took it to New Delhi Railway Station, where I got the reservation for my 2880-kilometre journey to Kottayam the following morning.

I then put in a call to Bhullar's office. The big man was not in, so I asked his secretary to tell him that he was not to worry about my problem, as it had been solved.

Late that evening Bhullar phoned me up. He was curious to know how I had pulled off the trick. I told him. He remarked that he was glad for me, but sorry I had not given him a chance of doing me a service.

'The Malabar Coast of South India has lots of ancient temples, churches, synagogues and mosques,' he added. 'Don't miss the Snake Park in Madras. And a trip to Kanya Kumari, earlier known as Cape Comorin, is a must – even Marco Polo spent some time at that spot. Many people consider it holy to watch the sunset there – a glorious spectacle, anyway. And make a point of bathing at the *triveni*. It's the place where the Arabian Sea, the Bay of Bengal and the Indian Ocean meet . . .'

A couple of days after I had left for Kerala, Bhullar announced to all his friends:

'And the things I arranged for him. I even got him the ticket and gave him any amount of advice and tips, so that no way can he go wrong.'

I learned about this on my return to Delhi.

'Bhullar specially made a date with me to tell me that,' Fikr told me then. 'He thought I didn't know how it really was.'

The Long Ride to Kottayam

The sky over Delhi was grey that February morning. I took a taxi to Hazrat Nizamuddin Station. When I got out it was pouring with rain. The station, only a few years old, looked washed and trim. On one platform there was a sign in Urdu:

RUMOUR-MONGERS ARE THE COUNTRY'S ENEMIES

Who was spreading what rumours against whom, I wondered. As I went up the foot-bridge leading to my platform, I caught sight of another sign, this time in Hindi:

OVER-PRODUCTION IS OUR SLOGAN

I wished luck to the anonymous optimists behind the slogan. Then I hurried over to the waiting 'J. J. Express', which takes some ten hours longer than the other express trains to reach Kerala.

The carriage in which I was to spend the next fifty-odd hours had a notice painted over its door, describing it as a 'three-tier sleeper-cum-sitting coach'. Going in, I saw what that meant. A passage ran down the length of the carriage. To its right were doorless compartments. Each of them had three bunks on either side, with two ceiling fans and two windows. I had a window seat on the left of the corridor, directly facing a compartment. Opposite me, by the adjoining window, sat a gentleman in a light suit. He was of medium height, in his late forties, with sensitive features and a good physique.

He flashed me a smile and, pointing to the first of the two bunks above the windows, said:

'That's my berth, but you can leave your luggage there for the day.'

I thanked him and set about depositing my things. A card attached to the handle of his suitcase on the bunk read: Reverend Joseph Pathuk. He apologized for occupying a place that actually belonged to me too.

How was that? He explained that the two seats fitted into each other

21

to make a bed for me at night. Asked, I mentioned my destination. A business trip? No, a private one to see a friend. Had I been to those parts before? No, it was the first time.

'Kerala has no winter, only some two months of the monsoons,' he told me. 'Its climate throughout the year is almost the same, with the temperature varying from 27 to 32 degrees Centigrade.'

Glancing at the heavy tweed jacket I was wearing with a jersey shirt and polyester trousers, he added:

'You won't be able to keep these clothes on when you get there.'

I looked about me. The carriage was only half full. The passengers appeared to be all South Indian. Laughter and Malayalam speech came from the neighbouring compartment, probably from a group of relatives or friends. The women, dark and young, had their hair hanging free over their shoulders; a red or black dot adorned the middle of their foreheads. The vivid colours of the men's shirts and ankle-length loincloths caught your eye. People were settling down for the journey ahead and had already spread their bedclothes on the bunks.

There was a whistle no louder than a sigh, with the train setting off as quiet as a cat. Soon a boy with a rag and a shoe-brush emerged from the next carriage. 'Polish, sahib; boot polish!' he cried as he marched down the passage. After him came another who sold cigarettes and matches from a tray suspended in front of him by a strap round his neck. Close on his heels followed a seller of writing materials. I let myself be talked into buying a ballpoint pen, about 30 centimetres long, tipped with a back scratcher.

Then two attendants in white appeared, carrying two large, drum-shaped metal containers. From a tap near the bottom they poured out tea or coffee into plastic cups. These drinks, I found out, would be served every few hours from early morning to late evening. My neighbour bought two coffees, offering me one.

In reply to my question he said that, like me, he was going to Kottayam. No, he didn't live there, but in a place a couple of hours away by bus. I learned that Kottayam, a centre of the Syrian Christian community, is the headquarters of Kottayam District, which has a population of over two million. And the sea, was it far from there? Oh, no, one could get to the coastal town of Cochin in something like an hour.

Meanwhile both the attendants were collecting the empty plastic cups.

'What do you do with them?' I asked the one who had come for my cup.

'We re-use them,' he answered.

'You clean them with detergents?'

'We follow our kitchen rules.'

The tall chap who approached us wore a Southern Railway badge, saying: PANTRY CAR SERVICE. He was taking orders for lunch. 'Vegetarian or non-vegetarian?' he asked. My neighbour remarked that he found vegetarian food always safe on a journey. I entirely agreed with him. About noon I saw a man in the carriage passage with a badge on his bush jacket which said: TRAIN SERVER. Balanced on a pad on his head were eight to ten large stainless-steel trays. I received one with a glass of water. The lunch on the partitioned tray consisted of fried wheat cakes, called *puris*; baked aubergine; potato and pea curry;

boiled rice; yoghurt and lemon pickle. Afterwards my neighbour belched in compliment to the meal.

'It's 50 per cent cheaper than in an ordinary restaurant,' was his comment.

More passengers had got on at the last station, so that all the vacant places were taken. Among the newcomers were South Indian young women, who wore bright exotic ear-rings. And they were dressed in Punjabi *salwar* trousers, in saris, in long skirts, in regional costumes. Their clothes threw flashes of so many colours that I felt as if I were in a flower garden.

We were passing through the state of Uttar Pradesh. My window aroused my curiosity. It had the usual sheet of glass in a sliding frame, together with a shutter to keep out the sun. But it was also equipped, on the outside, with four horizontal iron bars, painted yellow. This was something I had not come across on other trains. The meaning became clear to me when danger threatened later that night. At the moment, however, I looked out at the changing landscape. Now there appeared bizarre hilly formations and stretches of scrub; now deep valleys and large hills with the occasional ruins of a stone fort. Then the ground levelled out. Small houses roofed over with red tiles dotted the plain. The sun was shining down and it felt very warm.

I became aware of someone standing beside me. It was a boy with a shaven head out of which bulged a pair of large eyes. He was pointing with his broom to a coin I had dropped on the floor. I made a sign to say I did not want it. He picked it up and started sweeping out the passage. No one seemed to mind the clouds of dust he raised. After a moment he reappeared, passing near each passenger in the hope of getting a tip. My neighbour looked up from a leather-bound Bible he had been reading.

'I saw your name on the tag tied to your suitcase,' I said. 'You're a padre?'

He nodded with a smile. There are about 18 million Christians in India, including some 10 million Catholics. A large part of them live in Kerala, making up a fifth of the state's population, which has a Hindu majority. I asked the priest if it were true that St Thomas had brought Christianity to the Malabar Coast.

He remarked that it was a fact supported by history, as well as tradition. 'St Thomas got to Kerala about a decade before St Paul went to Rome,' he added. 'Landing at the village of Cranganore in AD 52, he began winning converts to Christianity. There were about two hundred thousand Christians when Vasco da Gama arrived in Calicut, now called Kozhikode. They had been under the authority of the Patriarch of Antioch for thirteen hundred years. Thanks to the commercial contacts with Persia, Kerala Christians were using the liturgy of the Orthodox Church by the fourth century. Nearly half of them eventually joined the Catholic fold, owing to the missionary activity of the Portuguese from the sixteenth century onwards.'

It was past ten o'clock in the evening when I took down my luggage from my neighbour's bunk. I pushed it under the hard narrow bed I had made by putting the two seats together. Most of the passengers had brought along their own bedclothes. Wishing to travel light, I had omitted to do so. A fellow passenger remarked that I should have hired a mattress earlier from one of the train attendants.

'You may still be lucky if you try,' he added.

I went through several carriages. In one of them there were no bunks and people were asleep in strange, twisted positions on their seats. The attendant, a dark middle-aged man, was getting ready to bed down. He said I was too late. Then he gave a sigh of helplessness and removed a foam-rubber mattress from the next berth. It was partly damaged, but I had no choice.

Shortly before midnight we came to Bhopal, the capital of Madhya Pradesh state. Here several rifle-carrying policemen in khaki uniform entered the carriage. They went round inspecting the bunks and toilets. I spoke to one of them, a well-built young man.

'The police presence,' he said, 'is only for the safety of the passengers.'

'Are we really in any danger?' I asked.

He enquired where I came from and where I was going. I told him. Could he see my ticket? I showed it to him. His suspicions were set at rest.

In a polite, even friendly, tone he said that the police had been tipped off that an armed gang planned to raid the train. The area between Bhopal and Nagpur, the capital of Maharashtra state, was thinly populated, with a rocky terrain and dense forests. It was a nest of dangerous criminals: that was why the train windows had wooden shutters and iron bars. The robbers played tricks with the railway signals or got one of their gang to pull the communication cord. When the train stopped outside a station, nobody was allowed to unlock a door and leave, even if they happened to live close by. The bandits might use this opportunity to get on to the train and rob people at knife-point.

'What do you do in such cases?' I asked.

'We have orders to open fire,' the policeman replied.

'How many people can you hit with a single round?'

'Twenty-five. My gun is fitted with telescopic sights and has a range of 3,000 metres. It fires ten rounds without reloading.'

'Have you ever had occasion to use it?'

A shadow crossed the policeman's young pimply face; he hesitated. 'Hm,' he said. 'Once.'

'You do create a feeling of confidence. How long will you be with us?'

'I'm on duty till four in the morning, when another colleague will take over,' he said, moving on.

The Reverend was looking at me from his bunk.

'Well, what do you think?' I asked him.

His smile, though gentle, was sceptical.

'The police act only after the event,' he remarked.

'Can there be trouble?'

'For the next five or six hours we're going to be in a danger zone. But let's put our trust in God and hope for the best.'

The window shutters had been lowered. I felt a little uneasy, wondering about the chances of an attack by the robbers. I split up my money into several portions. I put some bank notes in the hip pocket of the trousers I had on; a few more in my shoes which I pushed well back under my bed; a third lot in a hole I fortunately discovered in the mattress; and the fourth in the slightly torn lining of my suitcase. Trusting to luck, I then fell into a sleep broken by the occasional sounds of the policemen's boots.

'Well, how did you rest?' the Reverend asked me in the morning.

During the night I had tried to use my terry-cloth dressing gown as a blanket.

'All right,' I said. 'It did get a bit chilly though.'

I had reconverted my bed into two seats. The Reverend perched on the other one, sipping his coffee. We had safely made our way through the danger zone. The train was standing still. I looked out. The name of the station was Balharshah. We were in Maharashtra state. The platform was bathed in brilliant sunshine. Two signs – painted in large red letters in English – attracted my attention. One said:

DELAY BREEDS CORRUPTION

and the other ran:

COURTESY KEEPS EVERYONE HAPPY

'How do they strike you?' I asked the Reverend, indicating the signs.

'I doubt if anybody takes any notice of them,' he said.

Across the platform, under the roof of the station building, a section of a railway line hung from a crossbar. A man in khaki clothes hit it with a length of iron, producing a gong-like sound; then he waved a green flag and the train moved off. One of my fellow passengers came up to me.

'Where are you going?' he asked.

I told him.

'What's the purpose of your journey?'

'Seeing friends,' I said.

'Why aren't you travelling with your family?'

'I'll do so next time.'

'What business are you in?'

'Income tax law.'

The gentleman was one of several who asked me such questions. Once I had satisfied their curiosity, they were ready to tell me all I wanted to know, no matter how personal.

It was not midday yet. The weather had changed. My jacket felt much too heavy and I was sweating all over. By afternoon we were in the state of Andhra Pradesh. The ceiling fans, behind their wire guards, were going full blast. A hot wind blew in through the windows. At Dornakal Junction, hawkers of combs, hair ribbons, scents, fruit and sweets got on. One of them was selling a reddish-looking whisky in half-pint bottles. I shook my head when he approached me. He reduced his price by 20 per cent. The Reverend gave me a look that seemed to say I had better not buy the stuff.

'Kerala isn't dry,' he explained. 'you can get good whisky there.'

A group of wandering singers came into the carriage later that evening. To the accompaniment of some folk instruments, they filled the place with their rich musical voices.

'They're all of them blind,' remarked the Reverend, 'and yet how joyfully they sing!'

As we passed through Tamil Nadu state the following morning, it got even warmer. Neat little villages flashed by, with white houses, their courtyards planted with coconut palms and bananas. In the

distance stretched an unbroken line of mist-blurred hills. The train made a longish stop at Coimbatore, an industrial town in the Nilgiri Hills. I remembered its name from my student days: it was from Coimbatore that a muscleman by the name of Professor Rama Rau had sent me a prepaid postal course in body-building. I stepped off the train. The station had a well-kept look. On the platform were vegetarian and non-vegetarian refreshment stalls. I bought some food: it was piping hot and served on a large firm plantain leaf. The heat did not penetrate through the leaf to your hand, though you felt it all the more in your mouth as you ate.

Then we were off again. Soon we approached the Gap, where the slopes of the Western Ghat mountain range give access to the coastal strip of Kerala. I was struck by the beauty of the landscape – coconut groves as far as the eye could see. The warm red of the earth contrasted with the vivid green of the tall trees. The lakes and streams seemed endless.

I contemplated the vast stretches of ground covered with palmyra trees. They grow wild and are usually planted to mark land boundaries. They differ from the other palms in being fan-shaped with a crown of large leaves. In earlier times, the palmyra leaves were stitched together and written on with the point of a needle. They were used for book illumination as well, and even today palm-leaf painting is considered a popular art. The palmyra sap is, moreover, the source of jaggery, a coarse, brown sugar. The tree is also used for thatch, matting and timber.

The houses here looked different from those in North India. I asked the Reverend why most of them had peaked roofs.

'It's the famous Malabar Gable, a characteristic of Kerala

architecture,' he explained. 'The monsoon rains roll down the sloping sides, and the shape of the roof provides extra space near the top for storing coconuts and other products.'

The train was now moving through thick teak and rosewood forests – tropical forests cover about a third of Kerala's area. Then came rice and sugar-cane fields, coconut groves, spice gardens and rubber plantations.

I recalled that Roman trade with the Malabar Coast was at its height between the first century BC and the second century AD. In exchange for gold, the Romans bought ivory and sandalwood, scents and spices, pearls and textiles, elephants and monkeys, peacocks and parrots. Pliny the Elder (*c.* AD 23–79) was critical of the trade with India since it drained 550 million sesterces from the Roman treasury each year.

Nevertheless, there were fairly large Roman settlements along the Malabar Coast, as the excavations at Arikamedu, called Padouke by the Romans, have shown. And a temple to Augustus was put up at the port town of Muzyris in the first century AD. The Roman coins found in South India are mostly of Augustus and Tiberius.

We had to change trains at Ernakulam. As we waited there for the connection, I mentioned the beggars and cripples we had seen on the way from Delhi. What was one to do in the face of such tragedy?

'Do your duty and be good to others,' said the Reverend.

In about an hour we came to our journey's end at Kottayam. The Reverend asked if I would be all right. I told him that someone was meeting me off the train. We shook hands, wishing each other well.

I had not been on the platform for more than five minutes when I noticed two young men, one athletic, the other delicately built, both of whom had long moustaches. They fixed their eyes on me, then moved on.

A moment later I saw them walking back towards me.

Friends and
Strangers

As the two young men drew near, I thought they might be looking for me. They stopped a couple of feet away and asked me whether I was Mr Nath.

'Yes,' I acknowledged with relief.

They introduced themselves. They were from the Indian Institute for Regional Development Studies. Professor Varghese, my friend currently in hospital, had asked them to meet me. They would now take me to the room that had been booked for me.

Joseph, who was rather well built, picked up my suitcase. And Krishnan, thin and small, persuaded me to let him carry my brief-case. We went over a foot-bridge and at the barrier a tired and impatient collector snatched the ticket out of my hand.

Sunshine scattered like gold dust in the station forecourt. We threaded our way through the stream of traffic to a parking lot. A plump, grey-haired man stood beside a black Hindustan car. He was Professor Mathew, a colleague of Varghese's and, as I learned later, a former Member of Parliament. He greeted me cordially, then got in next to the chauffeur, while I sat between Joseph and Krishnan on the back seat. We drove to the city centre, whirled past the General Post Office and turned down a side street which was so narrow that I could not help thinking of Rome, where lovers in many of the houses need only to lean out of their windows to kiss.

The street ended in a broad rectangular stretch of ground. We got out in front of a large double-storeyed building. A sign above the entrance read KAYCEES – a phonetic spelling of the abbreviation KCs. Mathew left, saying he would see me when I came to visit Varghese at the hospital the following day. Joseph and Krishnan led me into the hall, where I checked in at the reception desk.

The clerk was a slim, agile man with a moustache. He put aside the register I had signed and turned to a key-and-letter rack on the wall behind him. It was flanked by two framed pictures of Christ. The first showed him with his disciples at the Last Supper; the second depicted him looking down a cypress-studded hill at the valley below. The bright gold of his flowing curls stood out in sharp contrast to the jet-black of the clerk's swept-back hair. When the man faced me again, I noticed the ivory cross he wore on a chain round his neck. So he was a Christian, and Kaycees probably stood for Kerala Christians.

'Please keep this with you for the duration of your stay here,' he said as he handed me a small brass key. 'It has no duplicate. And be sure to lock your room before going out.'

A flight of stone stairs brought us to a spacious basement. There were rooms on either side of the long, winding corridor. I turned the key in the lock, then pushed open the door. It was a large, high-ceilinged room. A three-barred window looked out on a narrow court-yard with several overfull dustbins whose lids did not shut. Joseph had switched on the ceiling fan at full blast. I freshened myself up in the adjoining bathroom.

'What's the temperature now?' I asked Joseph.

He thought it must be 28 or 29 degrees Centigrade.

'It should be about 10 degrees in Delhi,' I remarked.

'Really?' said Joseph. 'Fantastic.'

'Simply fantastic,' echoed Krishnan.

I asked them out to tea. Darkness had fallen, though the street-lights were not on yet. Our restaurant was on the upper floor of a building. The manager sat at his cash desk in a corner by the door, so you could not enter or leave without passing him. The overhead fans were all turning. The place was almost full; the moustaches of the men gleamed in the indirect lighting. We did find a table, though. I asked my companions about Varghese. He had received a transfusion and both had given blood for their professor the previous day. The operation had been a success.

I asked what they intended doing after their studies. Krishnan was an MA student; Joseph was reading for a PhD.

'I want to work at the grass-root level, educating and awakening people,' said Krishnan, running a comb through his wavy, neck-length hair for the fifth or sixth time since we had been there. 'Poverty can only be removed if power withers away from the bourgeois leaders in India. I'm sure it can be done. Three per cent of the people own all the wealth of the country. This has to be put into the hands of the 97 per cent.'

'You can't change things overnight,' put in Joseph.

'Change them I will, even if it takes me all my life,' retorted Krishnan. 'I can't stand people who lead a selfish, aimless existence.

31

Do you know, Mr Nath, we have lots of hippies in the south. Just why do they all come here?'

'They want to see the world on the cheap while they are young, that's why,' Joseph cut in.

'But they live without morals. Smoking charas – cannabis – is all that interests them. They should work for the masses, wage a war on hunger and poverty.'

'The masses in Europe are better off than those here,' said Joseph. 'And besides, most hippies are as poor as a church mouse.'

'You defend them because you yourself come from a rich family,' commented Krishnan. 'But deep down you know that I'm right. The only difference between us is that you are an armchair socialist whereas I'm a practical one.'

The waiter was hovering expectantly over us.

'Tea?' I said aloud. Then, looking up at the rotating fan: 'Rather warm here. How about something cold?'

'Do you know, Kerala isn't dry,' said Joseph.

I suggested beer. Joseph nodded his assent, but Krishnan seemed to hesitate. So I asked if he cared for a soft drink. Instead of replying, he looked round the restaurant with an air of uncertainty.

'He is afraid of being caught drinking beer,' Joseph told me, 'because technically he is an orthodox Brahman.'

'Rubbish!' Krishnan snapped out. 'I attach absolutely no importance to my belonging to the topmost caste. It's only that I don't want to hurt my mother's feelings.' His glance drifted to one of the booths that ran along the wall to our left which was unoccupied. 'If we could go in there,' he murmured.

'But of course,' I said, getting up.

The waiter brought us beer in the booth, together with a light supper I had ordered for myself. Krishnan drank half the beer in his glass at a draught, smiled sheepishly as Joseph winked at him, then wiped the froth off his moustache.

'My mother is a strict vegetarian,' he remarked as if he owed me an explanation. 'We never cook meat at home – not even eggs. Alcohol in any form or shape is taboo. She's a widow and a very sick woman. Being her only son, I don't want her to know.'

Joseph asked me about my programme. I told him the date by which I had to be back in Delhi. He mentioned the difficulty of getting a railway booking. I gave an account of my ordeal: how I had finally wangled a seat by producing my passport to prove that I was resident abroad. He raised my hopes. Professor Mathew had already said he would use his influence to book me a ticket from Kottayam. The outcome should be known the next day. If it was negative, I would have to book from Trivandrum as soon as possible – my passport should do the trick.

'Why do most men, including those quite young, wear a moustache here?' I asked as we were leaving the restaurant.

'It's a symbol of manhood,' said Joseph.

And Krishnan confirmed the statement with a nod.

'You don't often see it in Delhi – or the North generally. Except for the Sikhs, who have a religious reason, the majority of males there keep a shaved upper lip these days. Can it be possible that people in the South still cling to old-fashioned notions?'

This started an argument we were not to conclude that evening.

It was nearly eight o'clock now. I returned to my room at the Kaycees. I heard the whine of a mosquito and then the buzz of a fly at close range. Moths circled the overhead light. Then I realized that my bed only had a single sheet. I needed another to cover myself with. How on earth was I to get hold of one? In the corridor I bumped into an attendant. A tall man with a moustache that gave him a haughty appearance. I asked him into the room. He stared uncomprehendingly at me when I explained what I wanted. I tried gesticulating to bring it home to him.

'This no hotel,' he stammered out in English. 'Each bring his own sheet.' And he went away, leaving me frustrated.

Then I saw that the door of the room opposite to mine was open. I thought it was a linen room or an office of some sort, so I just walked in. Looking at the twin beds at the other end, I bumped into a table. On it stood a bottle of beer with a couple of glasses and a plate of cashew nuts. Two men sat by it, one with a twirled moustache. He was as black as ebony and his thick hair glistened oilily.

'Would you please come and take a look at my bed for a moment?' I asked him.

'I'm not a room boy!'

I nearly winced at his sharp tone.

'I didn't mean to offend you,' I apologized. 'It's just that I can't make myself understood to the attendant. Perhaps you could say a couple of words to him.'

The man glared at me with his big, brown eyes. He wore a singlet over a pair of shorts. His body, tightly knit, was all muscle. Embarrassed by his silence, I hastily withdrew. Then I unpacked my things. The wardrobe behind the bed creaked as I hung up a suit in it. A chest of drawers was wedged in next to a steel-legged table. I opened the top drawer and chased away a great red cockroach. After having a shower, I decided to go for a walk.

As I was locking my door, the man who had snubbed me earlier came out of his room. Muscles was the nickname I had given him. He invited me in. He now radiated charm and was full of smiles that showed the peeled-almond whiteness of his perfect teeth. He offered me a seat, then a cigarette, then a glass of beer.

'I saw you as you were checking in,' he said. 'Which is your home-town?'

I told him. What did I do? Income tax law, was my stock reply.

'How long will you be staying here?' he asked.

'I don't quite know yet. By the way, do you generally keep the fan on all the while you're in the room?'

'Yes, otherwise one can't breathe,' he said. 'The fan certainly makes the air a bit bearable, but it doesn't lower the temperature.' A short pause, then: 'Are you alone? I mean . . . Have you any friends here?'

'I hope to make some.'

'You'll meet very nice people here,' he remarked, topping up my glass. And he told me where I could buy beer at that time of night.

I thanked him.

'I remember seeing you with a camera,' he suddenly said. 'What make is it?'

'German.'

'Oh, German! German cameras are very good. You're lucky to have one. They are terribly expensive in India. Where did you buy yours – here or abroad?'

'It's not mine,' I replied, and this was true. 'A friend lent it to me.'

Muscles burst out laughing.

'Don't be afraid, I'm not going to steal it,' he said. 'More beer?'

I declined, with thanks. He got me to accept another cigarette, though. All the while, the other man at the table had not put in a word. Good-natured and unshaven, he nodded and grinned now and then. As he seemed to be fully at home there, I thought he must be my host's room-mate.

'I've a feeling that you are an educated man,' Muscles was saying, his eyes curiously resting on my face. 'I want to have a talk with you. See you in your room at eleven tonight. OK?'

As I gave a vague nod and stood up, he added: 'Oh, do keep your window shut at night – because of thieves, you know.'

I left the Kaycees and strolled down the main street with its brightly lit shops. Before long, however, I lost my bearings. I was standing uncertainly at the corner of a little side street when a turbaned giant, a Sikh, loomed up.

'*Sat siri akal*,' I said as he drew near.

This was a Sikh greeting, which means 'the true timeless being' –

God. The sound of his mother tongue in the faraway south made the man stop in his tracks.

Then he returned the salutation and shook hands with me. In a hearty, booming voice he said he had been living in Kerala for the past twelve years. Doing what? Oh, he was in the textile business. How did he like it here? Neither the food nor the climate was to his liking, but one had to earn one's bread – besides, Keralans were a friendly sort. When he learned where I was staying, he remarked that he lived just down the road and was almost my neighbour. I asked if there was a bar nearby. He said there was one only a couple of minutes from the corner.

'But the beer here goes to your legs rather than to your head,' he warned. 'I always stick to rum. It's the only local drink that has a kick in it. If I may give you a piece of advice – and I speak from experience – have a glass or two of rum whenever you want to feel good and happy.'

We bade each other good-night.

'My name is Dara Singh,' he shouted to me, suddenly turning round. 'Room number five – at the Besthotel. Call on me any time you need my services.'

The street down which I went was so badly lit that I had to grope my way until I came to the sign: Wine Shop. The place sold no wine, however; only spirits and beer. A bar had been built onto the front of the shop and there was a cell-like room at the back, with a black Madonna looking down from one of its walls. The customers were standing or seated, each with a drink in his hand. A loud buzz of voices. A chap of about 18 was tending the bar. I ordered a rum. He threw me a sharp glance.

'Your naughty place?' he asked in broken English.

I did not understand, so I pretended not to have heard him.

'Your naughty place?' he repeated.

Then it dawned on me that he meant my 'native place'. He was watching me with such curiosity that I could not find it in myself to disappoint him.

'Delhi,' I told him.

He poured me a shot from a bottle of whisky.

'Delhi very good,' he said, pushing the glass towards me.

'But I want rum,' I said.

'Rum no good,' he said. 'Whisky very good.'

Was it because of what my chance acquaintance Dara Singh had said a moment before? Or was it because the brand of whisky served seemed unfamiliar to me? Anyway, I pushed the untasted drink back towards the bartender.

'I asked for rum,' I said firmly.

The other looked displeased. As he eventually handed me my rum, he said:

'Delhi no good.'

When I went back to the Kaycees, the reception clerk said there had been a phone call for me. Asking me to wait a moment, he reached for the telephone pivoted on a circular metal plate over the counter. He turned it round and, checking something on a slip of paper, dialled a number, then handed the receiver to me. It was Joseph at the other end of the line. He had promised to give me a ring later in the evening. He told me that he would collect me at ten in the morning on the way to the hospital.

I asked the clerk to wake me at six. Could one have coffee at such an early hour? He replied that coffee was available from five onwards. I headed for the basement. A single lamp burnt in the corridor. The room facing mine was shut; no light shone under the door. It was already ten o'clock. Muscles must have gone to sleep, after all that beer he had been drinking. Or maybe he was out with his room-mate somewhere.

It had been a mistake to follow the advice given by Dara Singh, the friendly Sikh. The rum I had drunk at the bar was adding to the strain of my long journey. The fan was revolving fast above me. I bolted the window – 'because of thieves, you know', as Muscles had put it. I left the bedside lamp on as I lay down. My limbs felt heavy. I shut my eyes, but my eyelids burnt and a tingling in my legs kept me awake. I took a sip of water: it tasted flat, lukewarm. The air in the room had become dry. I switched off the fan. In no time I was soaked with sweat. I put it on again. I dozed off, only to be startled by a noise. Someone was knocking on my door and rattling its handle. What, morning already? My watch showed a little past eleven. So it must be Muscles. He had threatened to look in. The bedside light was on and the fan was whirring: no doubt he knew I was in. But I felt tired, exhausted. No, I was not going to face him now.

Then I heard the steps go back and the door of the room opposite slam shut. About half an hour later I was again aware of the door handle being jerked up and down. Muscles, it seemed, was trying to force an entry. Why was he behaving like a maniac? And why was he keen on seeing me at this time?

The rest of the night was far from peaceful. I was bitten by mosquitoes. I kept turning the fan off and on. And I had a running nightmare in which someone repeatedly hammered at the door and made frantic efforts to wrench off its handle. The man from reception had to knock long and hard, shouting: 'Six o'clock – six o'clock!' I woke up, feeling as if I had not slept at all. I swallowed an aspirin, shaved, showered. Meanwhile an attendant had brought me a coffee. It refreshed me. I did some writing. I was hungry now. Suppose I ran into Muscles, what excuse should I offer? I decided to say I had taken sleeping pills and did not hear him knocking.

'Could you suggest a place for breakfast?' I asked a man at the reception desk.

'Brahman or military, sir?'

'Pardon?' I gave the other a puzzled look, 'brahman' being connected in my mind with a Hindu of the highest caste. 'I'm not a member of the armed forces.'

The man smiled indulgently.

'It's got nothing to do with the army,' he said.

'What does it mean, then?'

'Brahman refers to a vegetarian restaurant, and military refers to a non-vegetarian restaurant.'

The place he directed me to was close by. A dreamy-eyed waiter approached me in a leisurely manner. I asked for the menu. An amiable grin exposed his yellow, horsey teeth.

'Try bull's-eye,' he recommended.

'What is that?' I said.

'Something you'll enjoy. If you are not satisfied, I will pay.'

'You seem to be a good salesman. Well, so be it. What should one drink with it?'

'Coffee, of course. I'll get you the best cup of coffee you ever drank.'

When he brought the order, I said:

'But it's merely eggs fried on one side!'

'That's not a nice name,' he said as if hurt by my remark. 'Bull's-eye sounds much better.'

The coffee was milky and much too sweet.

'I thought one got good coffee in Kerala,' I said.

'You don't like yours?' asked the waiter in astonishment.

'Why, it's the best I ever drank.'

I found Joseph waiting for me at the Kaycees. Was I late?

'On the contrary,' he replied. 'It's I who am a bit early. Remember our

37

discussion about moustaches yesterday? Well, I wanted to show you something.'

He drew a book from his brief-case and opened it at a place. It was a story in the form of a letter – *La Moustache* by Maupassant.

I glanced through the passages Joseph had marked. 'Really, my dear, a man without a moustache is not a man at all,' writes the heroine:

> Ah, a moustache is indispensable to a virile physique . . . Oh my dearest Lucie, never allow yourself to be kissed by a man who has no moustache; his kisses have no taste, none whatsoever! No charm, no spice . . . Well, without a moustache, kisses lose a great deal of their flavour and, moreover, they would be almost indecent. A lip without a moustache is like a body without clothes and you must always wear clothes – very few, if you like, but *something*. There is no love without a moustache.

I returned the book to Joseph, asking with a smile:

'What would be the number of moustached males among the local population?'

'I should say about 90 per cent,' was the prompt reply.

I stroked an imaginary moustache on my lip.

'It seems as if I will have to grow one pretty soon.'

'And it would look well on you, too,' Joseph remarked.

He then told me that I was to have dinner with him that evening. Varghese wanted me to be properly entertained. Had I ever tried toddy? No, I had only heard about it but would love to sample it. That, said Joseph, was splendid. We would taste toddy and some of Kerala's culinary specialities. He had spoken to a restaurateur he personally knew, so the food would be of excellent quality.

When I got to the hospital, Mathew was already there with his wife, a petite, graceful woman. By noon he would hear from Kottayam whether the booking to Delhi had been confirmed. He introduced me to some people around him. I was particularly drawn to a tall, double-chinned man with a light complexion – Professor Samuel. A local Jew, who ran a jam factory on the side, he had been to Oxford. He had also lectured in Sweden, the United States and elsewhere. A couple of observations he made on the Keralan scene impressed me and we agreed to meet later for a chat.

I was taken to the room where Varghese lay, covered with a sheet up to his chest. In London he used to sport a Castro-type beard, but now he was clean-shaven. A tube attached to his nose was connected to a larger one to draw off waste matter. He had been operated on for stomach ulcers. His dark hair contrasted with the white of the pillow.

A nurse sat on a stool in a corner. Part of the room was screened off as a place for his elder brother – many Indian hospitals allow someone from the family to stay with the patient.

When he saw me Varghese gave a faint smile. I touched his hand. His freckled arm looked thin.

'Glad you came,' he said weakly. 'Hope my friends are taking good care of you.'

I nodded. We spoke of some friends we had in common. He had remarried and his wife, Mary, was teaching at a college in Jaipur, Rajasthan. They had an 8-year-old son. He asked me to stay till the following Friday, by when he would be much stronger. I told him how Mathew was trying to get me a booking for my return journey.

'If he fails,' he said, 'you'll have to go to Trivandrum, unfortunately.'

The large hospital courtyard was laid out with trees, shrubs and flowers, and was nice and cool. The sunlight intensified the green of the foliage. Professor Samuel and I strolled down one of the little paths. I remarked on the charming setting.

'This is an exception,' he said. 'Generally, the Keralans have no eye for natural beauty. They often build a house with its back to a lovely view.'

I asked him about the popular regional-language press.

He paused in thought, resting his hand on his slightly bulging belly for a moment.

'The Malayalam magazines,' he told me, 'contain fiction that is full of cruelty. The drawings accompanying the stories make you feel that the artists hate the whole of humanity, especially children and old people. The accent on brutality is very strong. I was recently talking to the editor-in-chief at the Manorama Publishing House, which owns the bulk of magazines and newspapers in Kerala, including the top-circulation ones. He admitted that they had to bring out stories of violence to keep up the sales.

'And the odd thing is,' he went on, 'that the women in the illustrations are always fair, never dark. You'd think they were European women dressed in Indian clothes.'

I mentioned the blond Christ in the pictures at the Kaycees. Were any of the Kerala Christians blond? He knew of none. In that case, how did they identify themselves with their Messiah?

Samuel smiled:

'Christ himself was probably black, being a Jew.'

'Are there many Jews in India?'

'They're the tiniest religious group in the country.' Samuel brought together the fingertips of his right hand as if to illustrate the numerical smallness. 'Less than twenty thousand throughout India and barely two hundred in Kerala. And yet they're split up into exclusive sects. You have the Black, the White and the Slave Jews. Until recently the Slave Jews, who are often treated as untouchables, were not allowed to enter the synagogues of the other two sects.'

'How did they get these names?'

'I happen to be a White Jew. We're supposed to have a fairer skin than the Black Jews, though sometimes it's the other way round. They probably came here after AD 70, when the Romans sacked Jerusalem. We, on the other hand, arrived from Spain, frightened by the Inquisition.'

'What about anti-Semitism in Kerala?'

'There has never been any,' declared Samuel. 'The Black Jews, for instance, got special privileges from the fourth-century Hindu ruler of Malabar, as shown by three copper plates of that period which you can still see in Cochin. And when the Portuguese came and started giving hell to the White Jews who were settled on these shores, it was the Hindu Maharaja of Cochin who protected these persecuted people. He gave them land on which they built the Paradesi Synagogue in 1568. It was rebuilt a century later and is attended to this day – by the way, it is famous for its Old Testament scrolls. When you make a trip to Cochin, you must see the cemetery at the back of the Jewish quarter: it's called *Beth-haim*, or house of life. The oldest tombstone there dates back to 1688 . . .'

On the way back from the hospital I stopped at the General Post Office. I wrote a telegram at a desk against the wall. Behind me was a counter selling stamps. A customer there was having a heated argument with the woman clerk behind the grille. It seemed that he had overpaid for some stamps he had bought. The clerk was blaming him for not having checked his change immediately. As he turned away from the window, there was a look of anger and disgust on his face. He saw me observing him. This appeared to increase his irritation and he stared at me in a challenging way. I beckoned him to come closer. When he had taken a step towards me, I pointed to the first of the two signs in English that were displayed above the desk. It read:

COURTESY IS A SOLVENT OF THE CAUSES OF FRICTION

He shot a glance at it. I then drew his attention to the second sign, which ran:

THE REWARD FOR POLITENESS IS GOODWILL IN ABUNDANCE

So far he had not uttered a word. Now he exploded:

'You must be crazy to read such things.'

I made him a slight bow, then said:

'Thank you for sharing my fate.'

Leaving the post office, I walked along sun-baked streets, looking at shops. A number of pretty, well-dressed women were going about barefoot. In the morning, too, I had seen some high-school and college girls with nothing on their feet. It did not seem as if they could not afford to buy shoes or sandals. I found myself remembering a similar sight in London. It had been summer, said to be the hottest of the century, and almost everywhere you went, you came across barefooted young women. At each step they took, there came a tinkle from the bells they wore on their ankles. These musical instruments were, in fact, ordinary cowbells. An Indian business man had introduced them into England. I later bumped into him at a party, when he told me that he had made a million pounds from that transaction.

A message awaited me at the Kaycees: Mathew had not been able to fix me up with a booking; so I had better take a bus to Trivandrum tomorrow, buying my ticket today. The note mentioned several attractive places in and around Trivandrum I might try and visit. By the time I returned, Varghese hoped to have sufficiently recovered for us to have a real get-together.

The dinner appointment with Joseph was still an hour away. I decided to go and see about the bus ticket at once. On the way to the bus station I crossed the fruit and vegetable market. Bananas, mangoes, oranges, green coconut, pineapples, guava and jackfruit; tapioca, aubergines, bitter gourd, lotus stems and carambola; black pepper, ginger, cardamom, cloves, cinnamon, coriander, turmeric, red chillies . . . I was plunged into a world of colours and smells, emerging from it when I came to the ticket office. It was closed.

'Where is the booking-clerk?' I asked an official in one of the neighbouring rooms.

'Gone for a snack,' he said.

'When will he be back?'

'Soon.'

There was a refreshment stall next door. The counter was thick with flies, some of which had got under the gauze net spread over cakes and biscuits. I hung around the place until I saw the clerk arrive. He was a short, fat man with dyed hair. I told him I had been waiting for quite a while.

'Listen, my friend,' he said with a smile in his eyes. 'You had to pass through eighty-four hundred thousand forms of life before God created you a human being. He did not make you an Englishman or an American, but an Indian. Why? Because He wants you to achieve *moksha*, salvation. And to achieve that, you have to exercise patience. Patience and calmness are what every Indian should practise.'

'Yes, I'll do so in future.'

'Virtue, they say, is its own reward,' he said. 'All the same, I'll give you a window seat.'

I was back in my room when Joseph came, apologizing for the slight delay.

'Are you ready?' he asked. 'Shall we go?'

I got up. He wiped the sweat away from his forehead with his handkerchief.

'You'd be better off without your jacket,' he suggested.

I slipped out of the jacket, dropped it on the bed and followed him out.

'Our family car,' he explained as we settled ourselves in the back of a large, green Ford parked opposite the Kaycees.

The man at the wheel turned round and shook hands with me. He was tall and hollow-cheeked, with broad shoulders and a wiry body. Joseph introduced him as Muhammed, his chauffeur.

As we drove off, I asked him how it was that he, a Christian, had a Muslim chauffeur.

He smiled. 'Because Muslims and Christians have always lived in harmony in Kerala,' he said. 'And my parents are broad-minded in such matters. Besides, he is a superb driver. Do you know, he is a graduate.'

'A real one?'

'Yes, a genuine college graduate.'

'It's the first time I've been driven by a graduate chauffeur,' I said. 'What made him chose this job?'

'The simple fact that he has a wife, three children and his parents to support. He could find no other job. Among India's states we have the highest rate of literacy. But we have one of the highest rates of unemployment too. The number of educated people out of work is always rising. Many of them have gone out to the Persian Gulf, but those countries are now cutting down on the foreign labour they employ.'

Meanwhile we had reached the outskirts of the city. Coconut palms stretched away on either side of the even macadamed road. The car turned down a narrow trail, pulling up before a white-washed building in a clearing. It was a lightly built, one-storey structure, shaped like a shoebox. The interior, however, suggested plenty of space, and had several booths. We sat down in one of them. Its earth floor was covered with fine pebbles that crunched underfoot and were no doubt intended to imitate a beach. Straight-backed chairs flanked a long and bare wooden table in the middle.

We had scarcely taken our seats when the curtain over the booth door parted, revealing the proprietor. He was a big raw-boned man, not quite 30, in a khaki bush jacket worn over a white ankle-length garment, known locally as a *mundu*. There were handshakes. Joseph exchanged some words with him in Malayalam, apparently about the dinner awaiting us.

A young waiter came in with three bottles containing a milky-looking drink.

'Toddy!' announced Joseph.

He poured some into my glass and I tasted it.

'Well, how do you find it?' he asked.

'A bit sour,' I said, 'but smooth on the tongue.'

He filled up the glasses. After a sip from his, he pronounced it to be good fresh stuff. I enquired whether this fermented drink from the sap of coconut palms had any kick in it.

'It's not exactly water,' he replied. 'No doubt, it acts slowly, but it's strong; in spite of that, it leaves no hangover. Well, cheers!'

And he drained his glass, saying we were going to have a skinful tonight. Muhammed, our chauffeur, and I followed suit.

'Tell me,' I asked him, 'do you know any Urdu or Persian?'

Muhammed shook his head.

'Only Malayalam and English,' he said.

'Then what language do you read the holy Koran in?'

'Malayalam, my mother tongue. I am a Moplah.'

'What does that mean?'

'My ancestors were Arab traders who settled on the Malabar Coast in the ninth century. The other Malabar Muslims are merely Hindu converts.'

'Then you must know Arabic, being descended from the Arabs.'

'No,' he grinned, 'I don't.'

Muslims, like Christians, form almost one-fifth of Kerala's population. I asked Muhammed whether the Hindu–Muslim relations in the state were good.

'They have always been good,' he replied. 'We don't have communal riots here, as you have in the North. That is because the Arabs who brought Islam to the Malabar region didn't want to remain apart from the Kerala society.'

Three more bottles had appeared on the table. There were several types of fish: smoked, grilled, curried or cooked with grated coconut. At first I merely toyed with the food. I grew up in a North-Indian city thousands of kilometres

43

from the sea. I was 22 before I had tried any fish. Then, the bones that got stuck in my throat put me off it completely. Joseph laughed as he saw me picking at my food.

'It's child's play,' he said.

In a few minutes he had taught me how to eat fish with my fingers. It turned out to be an experience I found novel as well as delightful.

'Some 10 per cent of the women go about barefoot in Kerala,' Joseph said when I told him about what I had seen earlier in the day.

'They didn't look at all poor,' I said. 'On the contrary, they were well groomed and elegant. What can the reason be?'

'The hot weather here,' suggested Muhammed.

'And the Christian girls?' cut in Joseph. 'They wear shoes.' Then he turned to me: 'The barefoot women are all Hindus. Orthodox brahmans, as a matter of fact. Shoes are made of cowhide, and the cow is sacred to them.'

'The Muslims don't care for pigskin, either,' commented Muhammed.

'Why don't these Hindu women wear rubber sandals or canvas shoes?' I asked.

'They're just orthodox,' Joseph said. 'Some prejudices never die. The ladies believe that wearing shoes is a Western custom.'

Now came the *pièce de résistance*, served up by the proprietor himself. Joseph paid him a well-turned compliment. He asked what I thought of it.

'Delicious,' I said, 'but what is it exactly?'

'Take a coconut that is three-quarters ripe,' he said, illustrating the recipe with gestures. 'Then make a hole in it and insert prawns and spices. Seal up the opening. Coat the coconut shell with clay. Bake for something like three hours – till the coconut meat melts and mixes with the other ingredients. The result will be the delicacy before you, a Kerala speciality. I may remind you, at this stage, that toddy goes particularly well with this dish. So let's drink: first to the Arabian Sea for the prawns; then to the palms for the coconuts; again to the palms for the bottles of toddy; then to this green wonderland of ours for the spices, and then to . . .'

We drove back to the Kaycees a little after ten. The kitchen was still open, so I asked Joseph and Muhammed to have a cup of coffee with me in my room. They nodded.

When we got to the basement, the sight of my partly open door made me stop sharply. In the ray of light that fell from the corridor into the room, I saw my suitcase on the chest of drawers: it stood unzipped, with the top folded back. The toddy I had drunk so freely, left me. Clearheaded I realized what had happened.

'It's been broken into,' I said.

'Are you sure?' Joseph looked shocked. 'Why not check everything first?'

'Not necessary,' I murmured and swung round to the door opposite mine, but it was locked.

'But such things don't generally happen here,' he remarked. 'It's a Christian house.'

'It was Muscles,'

'Who do you mean?' Joseph wondered.

'Someone who was trying to break my door handle last night. Wait, I'll be right back.'

I ran up the stairs to the reception desk and was so out of breath that I could hardly speak.

'Yes, sir?' said the clerk. 'You want anything?'

'Where is that Muscles fellow?' I blurted out.

The other looked puzzled:

'A friend of yours?'

'Sorry,' I said, getting a grip on myself. 'I meant the big strong man in room number ten, directly facing mine.'

'Oh,' smiled the clerk. 'If it's Mr Ranjan you're looking for, he will be back next week.'

'Damn,' I muttered. 'Is there any way I can get hold of him at this time?'

'It might be rather awkward. Mr Ranjan is a circus man – a lion tamer. He is probably with one of his cats in a round cage right now.'

Without another word I made my way back to the basement corridor. Joseph and Muhammed stopped talking. They both looked worried. We went into the room. My camera lay above the pile of clothes in the suitcase. I picked it up, felt its weight in my hand, unbuttoned the case it was in: everything intact. Then I took up my wallet that had lain next to the camera: all the money I had brought from Delhi was still there.

'Anything missing?' asked Joseph.

I had got myself into such a state that I could only shake my head and bring out a hoarse 'no'.

There was a knock. An attendant came in with the coffee I had ordered. On the tray he carried there was something I had not asked for: a bottle of beer.

'Mr Ranjan left it for you before his departure last night,' he explained in reply to my questioning glance.

As we were drinking coffee, I saw my jacket still lying just where I had tossed it hurriedly in the afternoon. Casually I lifted it off the pillow on my bed. I must have made a sound of surprise, because Joseph anxiously asked:

'Anything wrong?'

'No–o,' I stammered, adding slowly: 'Everything's all right.'

I was too embarrassed to tell him that I had left the room key in the pocket of my jacket and that I had just found it again.

Later, when alone, I wondered what kind of man my neighbour Ranjan the lion tamer was. I felt I owed him thanks for the beer and an apology for not having opened the door to him the night before.

But it was getting on for midnight and I had to be up early so as not to miss the bus to Trivandrum.

Man Is Adaptable

The sun was yet golden and the air unoppressive at that hour of the morning. Three steps led to the veranda of the ticket-office at the bus station in Kottayam. On the middle step stood a man in spotless white, reading a newspaper held out in front of him. Directly above him, on the top step, another man was leaning over and going through the same paper. And a third man, bent double on the bottom step, gripped the lower end of the same paper and had his eyes glued to it.

I was still thinking of this tableau a couple of hours later when the bus stopped to let the passengers refresh themselves at a restaurant. I ate something and bought the *Hindu*, one of the major English-language newspapers of India. Then we set off again. Each of the long, bench-like seats on either side of the aisle had three people on it. At the front of the bus was a group of barefoot young women with flowers in their hair, which was worn in plaits down their backs. For a while I listened to their cheerful chatter, then looked out of the window. Suddenly a hand appeared under my nose, which belonged to the third man on our seat.

'Can I have your paper, please?' he said.

I thought fast. If I lent it to him, it would be impolite to ask for its return until he had read it, and that might take quite some time, depending on the items found interesting. It seemed to be a general practice here: people borrowed your paper, often without a 'by your leave', and kept it as long as they liked; the owners never objected – a strange kind of tolerance.

'Sorry,' I replied. 'I'm reading it.'

'But it's lying folded in your lap,' he declared.

That was true. In some embarrassment, however, I picked up the paper.

'I haven't done with it yet,' I told him.

The man bowed to me with a kindly look, withdrawing his hand.

47

I felt bad about my refusal, so touched was I by his humility. But the next minute I was relieved to see that he had got hold of a section of a newspaper from someone in the next row.

On reaching Trivandrum I made a dash for the railway station. I bought a ticket to Delhi and asked if I could travel on a particular day.

'In principle you can,' the booking-clerk said, 'but you need a reservation.'

'Can you give me one?'

'No; try the Divisional Office.'

'Is it far?'

'Not exactly far, but perhaps you'd better take a taxi.'

My suitcase was fairly heavy, so I went down one of the platforms and asked at a bookstall where the left-luggage office was. An oblong cardboard sign, hung on string, floated above the newsagent. Written in ink, it said in English on one side:

RAILWAY TIMETABLE NOT AVAILABLE

And on the other:

AVOID FREE READING

'Is it very widespread, this habit of free reading?' I asked the newsagent.

'Oh, yes,' he replied, taking a sip of tea from the cup in his hand. 'It is like an epidemic. This is a bookstall. But people like to think it is a public library.'

The left-luggage office was next to the bookstall. It consisted of two rooms, one opening into the other. Several travellers stood about in front of it. The clerk, in his late twenties, was bald but he had a bushy beard. He asked to see my ticket. He examined it slowly as if it were a fake. Then I had to fill out a form. The particulars to be answered included my name, my father's name, my age, my occupation, my address and the duration for which I wanted to deposit my luggage, namely one suitcase.

When I handed back the completed form, the clerk went over it with what was either extreme carefulness or absolute lack of interest. Then he put it down on his desk, opened his fountain-pen and poised it over the section for official remarks. He began writing something there, paused and seemed to listen to some shouts and laughter coming from outside the office. A dreamy look stole into his eyes, while an absent-minded smile played on his features. He put pen to paper again, only to lift it and strain his ears for the voices in the distance.

Subsequently I drove to the Railway Divisional Office, an imposing building with many rooms. I was directed to one of them, where the scratch of pens was the only sound I caught as I lingered hesitantly at the threshold, watching the three men inside. Two of them were almost hidden behind a stack of files and documents at the other end of the room. The third was near the door. The desk he was seated at was much bigger than theirs. It was a full minute before he looked up and favoured me with a glance of enquiry. I mentioned what I had come for.

'The reservation supervisor will see you soon,' he said, indicating one of the two vacant chairs placed against the wall to his left. 'Please wait.'

Then he lost himself in his papers again. He had a lion-like profile and looked well preserved in the dark suit he wore with a lemon-coloured tie fastened with a gold pin. After some twenty minutes he seemed to remember me.

'What can I do for you?' he asked, shifting in his chair to face me.

'I should like to put the matter to the reservation supervisor personally,' I said.

'You are speaking to him.'

I could hardly believe my ears. 'You mean to say . . .?'

'Yes, I am the reservation supervisor,' he explained with emphasis. 'Please state your case.'

I told him my story again.

'I've been in the Southern Railway all my life,' he remarked, 'and I've always observed the principle of fairness and justice. Now that I am nearing retirement, I'm not going to behave in a different way. You tell me that you live abroad and must be back by a certain time. That does not seem to be a valid reason for me to treat you as a special case. You should have made travel arrangements in advance. Why didn't you do so?'

'There are things over which man has little control,' I said, trying to put some pathos in my voice. 'One of my closest friends lives in Kerala – in Kottayam, to be exact. I hadn't seen him for ten years. Then I learned that he was seriously ill. So I rushed to his sick-bed. I couldn't bear to go away without visiting him. It was all so sudden.'

The official did not speak. He seemed to be thinking. I wondered whether I had touched the right chord. He cleared his throat once or twice.

'Could you write an application stating these circumstances?' he then said.

'But of course.'

He handed me a form. 'You must fill this up, too.'

When I had done both things, he told me I should confirm my booking on the day of my departure: the names of those entitled to travel would appear on a chart put up at the railway station an hour before the train left. I asked whether I might feel certain of my name being on that list.

'I promise that your case will be definitely resolved,' he answered with the air of a man whose word is not to be doubted.

'But positively, I hope?'

'You seem to be a suspicious sort of person.'

'On the contrary, I have full confidence in your willingness to help me.'

I collected my suitcase from the left-luggage office and hired a cab. I asked the driver where I could find a room. He suggested trying a place in Statue Street, near the Government Secretariat.

'Statue Street?' I smiled, amused by the name. 'Why is it called that?'

'Because it has the statue of a famous statesman of ours,' he replied.

'You seem to have a lot of statues here – at almost every street corner and crossroad. In no other part of India have I seen so many statues of poets, writers, social workers or political figures.'

'That's right.' His grin broadened. 'If you ask me I'll name each street in Trivandrum as Statue Street number so-and-so.'

I told him to stop for a moment at the Government Tourist Office. It was a single-room affair. The young official at the desk was smartly turned out. On the walls hung posters. The pictures of sunrise and sunset on the sea seemed amazingly alike. Down from some posters stared elephants, bison and tigers from the wildlife sanctuary at Periyar in Kerala's highland zone. I dropped into a chair across the desk. Next to me sat a blonde girl, who judging by her accent, was English.

The official shook his head with an air of distress. Behind him hung a large photograph of a pilgrimage centre in Trivandrum: the eighteenth-century Padmanabha Temple. The English girl, who wore a pale-blue blouse over grey jeans and nothing on her feet, was in her early twenties and remarkably good-looking.

'I am sorry,' he was telling her with as much charm as he could put in his voice, 'but the temple is barred to non-Hindus.'

'Isn't there any way to get in – for a couple of minutes, even?' she asked.

'There was a Japanese woman here about two years ago,' he said. 'She was an artist and wanted to photograph the interior of the temple. She succeeded, but only after she had changed her religion.'

'The Japanese are Buddhists, not much different from the Hindus,' said the girl. 'But I'm a Catholic, and Catholics can't change their religion . . .'

After getting the information I needed, I stepped out of the office and saw her coming out of the neighbouring bookshop. She wondered if I knew where she could exchange a book she had read. I remarked that, like her, I was new to the city. Which part of Britain did she come from?

'Devon,' was her reply.

'You're the second person I've met from Devon,' I said.

'Oh, indeed?'

'The first one was a girl too. Told me she worked on a chicken farm and could kill a hen with her bare hands.'

'Dear me!' She burst out laughing. 'I'm a vegetarian, though.'

'Really! What made you one?'

'I saw a documentary film about the way animals are slaughtered.'

'Don't you ever miss meat?'

'Oh, no! Being a vegetarian makes life a lot simpler. And it helps me get on with the brahman family I'm staying with at Kovalam.'

'At the seaside?'

She nodded.

'You must be a millionaire, then.'

Smiling, she mentioned the amount she paid for her lodging – a pittance. She was, I learned, a teacher. Her grandfather had been a postmaster in India. She had saved up for the present trip which had begun a month earlier.

'Sorry about the temple,' I said.

'I don't give up easily,' she remarked. 'I'll dye my hair black, put on a sari borrowed from my landlady and enter the temple like a Hindu woman.'

I wished her luck, then got back into the taxi, whose meter had been ticking away all the time. We turned off the main street, passing a big dark statue, and drew up opposite a signboard reading The Swapna Tourist Home.

Swapna means 'dream', so I asked the man at the reception desk:

'Is this a dream house or a place where people dream of home?'

The fattish, grey-headed man smiled a gold-toothed smile.

'You can sleep well here,' he said. 'No bedbugs, no noise, everything clean. You want a room? There is one free at the moment.'

Gratefully I signed the register.

The wall to the right of the reception desk displayed a framed watercolour of the beach at Kovalam. I asked him how to go there. He consulted a timetable and told me when and where I could catch the next bus if I hurried. I plumped down my luggage in my room and made my way to East Fort, a Trivandrum district named after the fort that contains the eighteenth-century temple and several palaces.

The bus station looked as large as a football field. Buses were parked, buses were coming and going. Clouds of dust shot up every so often, enveloping the posts with the timetables for various routes. The place

swarmed with people – the refreshment booths there could not complain about business.

It was already after four o'clock, but still quite hot. The bus was late The queue for it kept getting bigger and the people more restless. No wonder that the arrival of the bus threw things into confusion. Everyone charged at it as if afraid of being left behind. I, too, had to push, using my elbows. I even managed to bag a seat.

Then we got moving. The number of stops on the way seemed endless. At each of them more people got on. The fully packed, ancient bus creaked leisurely along. There was, however, never a dull moment. Arguments, laughter and an occasional song enlivened the journey that scarcely took half an hour.

In Kovalam I wandered through the residential quarter and then up a steep path to an asphalt road, bordered with tall coconut palms and white-painted metal drums buried in the ground. Then the Arabian Sea showed through a gap in the trees – a dazzle of pink under the late-afternoon sky. Shortly afterwards I found myself in a lush garden, with a hotel at its furthest edge. I went through the entrance hall, which was decorated in a blend of the traditional and the ultramodern. That could only mean one thing: the hotel charged fancy prices. Some foreign tourists, apparently staying there, added to the impression of the place being classy. As it was a warm day, they wore a minimum of clothes; not so, the Indian behind the reception desk, who in prim English answered my query about getting to the beach: he was got up in a double-breasted suit with a bow-tie.

A shop in the hall sold souvenirs and other articles. An elderly European man in shirt and shorts stood near the counter, with a motherly sort of woman by his side. They were, it seemed, perplexed by the contents of a cellophane packet he was turning over in his hand. He saw me buy a similar one.

'Excuse me,' he said with an American accent. 'Could you tell us what this is?'

'Banana chips,' I said.

'Wow!' he exclaimed. 'Banana chips. Never tried them. Are they any good?'

'Delicious,' I replied, 'But they're flavoured with chillies – very hot.'

He pointed his thumb at his stomach, shaking his head. 'Thanks for telling us.' And he handed the packet back across the counter.

This earned me a look that was far from grateful from the shop assistant. I answered with a gesture of helplessness.

The lifts were nearby; they only went down, though. I got into one, stopping it at each of the three floors below. Every time I did so I saw a brightly lit corridor between two rows of rooms, with not a soul around. There was an air of emptiness about the place, an air of desolation.

I had an uneasy feeling, almost claustrophobic, of being in a closed space. The feeling grew when, stepping out of the lift, I found myself in sudden darkness. I groped my way along a tunnel-like passage that soon ended in an outdoor terrace. The palm-fringed beach unfolded before me, extending indefinitely.

The sea sparkled in the distance. The warm, pale-yellow sand was ankle-deep. I tried to walk fast so as to reach the shore before dark. From a hut to my right a middle-aged European woman emerged in a green dress, carrying a swim-suit over her arm. I stood before a black oblong board supported by a pair of steel legs. Written with chalk across its middle was the water and air temperature for that day. A little ahead shone the red-and-white sails of two skiffs lying side by side on the sand.

The beach here was crescent-shaped. In the sea some youngsters – local boys, by the look of them – were playing about like dolphins, vanishing under the water and then popping up with excited cries. Beyond, a tiny motor boat, its bows tilted up at a steep angle, described circles. People stood about in knots on the beach, watching the sunset with a reverent expression on their faces. Then the great scarlet disc on the horizon slid into the sea. Some men and women struck up a song that sounded like a lullaby.

I sat down on the sand and turned up my trousers. A large wave with a big top rolled on to the shore. I jumped back just in time to prevent myself getting drenched.

'I beg your pardon,' I said, having collided with someone behind me.

The other, a well-knit man of about 40, dismissed the incident with a good-natured smile.

'What place do you come from?' he then asked in English.

He was not alone. With him were a moon-faced woman in a white sari as well as two boys and a girl in their teens. I had heard them talk in Hindi, so I replied:

'Like you, from the north.'

'And you are here without your family?' he asked in a tone of surprise.

'Yes,' I replied, assuming a look of regret. 'I'm on a business trip.'

'You would get more enjoyment out of it if your family was with you.'

'If you say so. Do you find South Indian food to your taste?'

'Some of it,' he spoke in a way that suggested that South Indian food did not make his gastric juices flow. 'But man is adaptable. As I was telling my family only this morning' – his hand made a graceful movement towards the members of his party – 'a highly developed man is one who is adaptable.'

Asking him to keep an eye on my sandals, I waded into the water. I saw a catamaran and a fishing boat floating up and down the waves some way off. The tepid bluish water rose above my calves to my rolled-up trousers.

'Why didn't you have a dip?' the man asked when I came back.

'I was warned against it at my hotel,' I explained. 'The manager told me that every month there were newspaper reports of bathers drowned or carried away by the undertow.'

He chuckled:

'But we have bathed here.'

'You have more courage.'

'I have a rather strong feeling for history. When I dived into the water, I became one with the glorious past of our country – because it was to these shores that people from faraway lands like Phoenicia,

Rome, Greece and Arabia sailed in ancient times. You too went and stood knee-deep in the sea, so you are now up to your knees in India's history. Wife,' he called out, though the moon-face was standing just beside him. 'Did you hear what I said? Up to the knees in history! Remind me to put it in my diary tonight.'

'Very good,' she said, nodding.

'Yours must be a witty diary,' I said.

'It's full of variety. Of that I'm sure. Whatever impresses me or my family goes into it. I'll give you an example.' He took a piece of paper out of the breast pocket of the open shirt he wore over his wide cotton trousers. 'Here, read this.'

The pencilled note ran:

KOVALAM BEACH CENTRE
MET. AND TIDAL INFORMATION

Day temperature	...	31.9
Night temperature	...	19.5
Sea temperature	...	25.1

The particulars were copied down from the notice-board I had seen a little earlier. I returned the note with thanks.

'Do you know why I want to enter this in my diary?' he asked.

'You must have a reason for it,' I said.

'I have – and an excellent one too,' he declared. 'I believe that the weather, like the stars, influences our lives more than we realize.'

A significant smile passed over his face, and the white of his teeth gleamed in the twilight.

'This diary of mine,' he added as if letting me into a secret, 'will form a human link between me and my descendants. My children will read it and relive the experiences I record. So will their children, and those that come after them. My little girl and both my boys keep a diary too. Am I right?' he asked, turning to the people he had mentioned.

'Yes, daddy,' they replied in chorus.

It was late in the evening when I returned to Trivandrum. I had something to eat at a snack-bar in the railway station before going through the booking-hall. The space between the first-class and second-class booking-offices was crammed with people waiting for their trains. Some stood or sat by their luggage; others lay on the beds they had made up on the floor. The fans fitted to the high ceiling were all turning. None of that, however, seemed to cool the atmosphere.

As I was about to make my way down the wide station steps into the street, a dark woman in a faded sari emerged from behind a pillar. On one arm she had what looked like a ball of white-ish wool; then I spotted a pink little tongue in the ball – a tiny puppy.

'Sorry,' I said as the woman asked for alms, 'I haven't got any small change.'

She continued standing with her hand held out. Obviously, she did not understand what I had said. I tried to explain with gestures. Eyes full of appeal, she stood there another moment. Then she walked over to a mat spread a couple of paces away on the floor. Before stretching herself out, she fingered the string the puppy had round its neck. Then she tied the other end to her wrist, put her head on the pillow and shut her eyes. The puppy remained on its feet for a bit, nestled up against her and seemed to fall asleep almost at once.

As the woman slept, her facial expression became young and tender. I was reminded of a story from my childhood which my father had told me. I do not remember what it was about, but I still know the exact words it ended with: 'Beggars can be givers too.'

Later that night, as I was unpacking my suitcase at the Swapna or Dream Tourist Home, a gap-toothed boy smiled at me from a brightly coloured portrait over my bed. In the glare of the unshaded lamp, I saw that the room had recently been decorated. The walls were painted a vivid green and the fittings seemed new. There was, however, not a single hanger in the wardrobe. A wash-basin with a tap was fixed to one wall, but the mirror that should have been above it was attached to the opposite wall.

Then I noticed cobwebs hanging from each corner of the otherwise clean, whitewashed ceiling. I switched on the overhead fan, making them dance in the swirling currents of air. Yet a layer of dust lay undisturbed on the stone shelf built into the wall on my right. It was a narrow shelf, about 30 centimetres long, with a framed copy of the 'Rules and Regulations' of the hotel resting upright on it.

I found the opening sentence of this document remarkable. It referred to the people staying at the establishment as customers rather than as guests. Most of the hotels, *pensions* and restaurants I remembered described those paying for their accommodation or food as guests – a term which, in such situations, seemed odd: as if a friend or a kindly stranger had invited you and you did not have to pay the bill on leaving. I had just read somewhere that an American restaurant in Boston presented its customers not with a bill but with a 'guest receipt'.

'Dream Tourist Home,' I murmured to the framed sheet of typewritten paper, 'you call a spade a spade. All the others should follow your example.'

Then I caught sight of the last clause of the 'Rules and Regulations'. 'Any kind of gambling or immoral activities', it ran, 'are prohibited. The management reserves the right of asking any customer (lodger) to quit the room at any moment without giving any notice and the customer (lodger) should vacate the house immediately.'

My enthusiasm suddenly subsided. The adjective 'immoral' occupied my thoughts. Did it mean sexual misbehaviour or anything one found unseemly? And the warning about being turned out of one's room 'at any moment' without notice really added up to this – that the poor customer was in fact entirely at the mercy of the Dream management.

Then I cheered up. In a few hours I would be off to Kanya Kumari (Cape Comorin). Most likely this clause of the 'Rules and Regulations' was no more than legal jargon for the sake of form on the dusty, yellowing paper.

A Missed Opportunity

Early next morning a motorized rickshaw dropped me opposite a large square near Trivandrum Station. It was warm again. Cut-open watermelons and coconuts, together with a variety of other fruits on sale, shone in the sun. The sight of sugar-cane being crushed in a small, mobile mill slowed my steps. When I was a student, I used to stop every day on my way to college for a spot of sugar-cane juice. Fresh from the mill, flavoured with lemon and ginger, it was served in a thin clay bowl that you threw away after use. Although I had not tasted the drink since then, I was now seized with a instant craving for it.

But I was pressed for time and carried on. I negotiated the crowds and the ranks of buses *en route* to the information and ticket booth,

where a notice said that only those who queued up would be attended to. A broad-shouldered Sikh in front of me had just had an argument with the clerk behind the booking window. Striking his ink-black beard, he now leaned towards the window till his turbaned head was touching the grille.

'Getting an answer out of you is like drawing a tooth,' he remarked in a loud, sugary voice to the clerk. 'Tell me, what's your problem? Did your wife run away with a neighbour last night?'

The other, a tense-looking middle-aged man, let out an angry exclamation. But the Sikh was gone, so he stabbed me with a vicious glance instead. Curtly he informed me that I would get a ticket from the conductor on the bus to Kanya Kumari. I enquired when the bus was due to leave and he told me to look at the timetable outside. And where would I find the bus? He replied with a vague, impatient gesture.

People were already getting on to the bus by the time I found it.

'Could you please assist me?' someone asked me.

I turned round and saw a compact little man; a blond beard framed his nut-brown face. He had an enormous rucksack on his back. I helped him carry it up the ladder and pack it, among other pieces of heavy luggage, on to the roof of the bus.

We set off shortly afterwards. He had a seat by the window. Above him a notice asked passengers not to spit or use bad language. I sat by his side. He looked out of the window at the changing landscape. His khaki jacket seemed to have a great many pockets, from one of which he took a slim volume with an English title, *A Guide to South India*. He lost himself in it. Occasionally he underlined a word or marked a place on a map in the book. Then he scribbled something in a diary. That done, he looked round, scratching his hairy throat with an air of relief.

'I am called Helmut,' he told me with a smile that lit up his fine blue eyes.

'The name is German,' I said. 'But your accent is American.'

'That is because I have many American friends,' he explained, adding that he was from near Munich in West Germany.

'Have you been in India long?'

'Long enough to have got an idea of this vast country.' He paused; then: 'I plan on going to Nepal next.'

'Surely you've been to many places?'

Yes, he knew most countries of Europe. Besides he had been in Vietnam early the previous year. Then he had hitched a ride to Rangoon, in Burma.

'I spent three delightful days on rice sacks in a lorry,' he added. 'Oh yes, I like Burma – love it, in fact. But as a foreigner I couldn't stay there longer than a couple of weeks at a time. I hope, however, to go there again this year.'

'Are you a journalist; do you write about what you have seen?' I asked.

'No.' He shook his head with emphasis. 'I have a job in the production department of a newspaper. But my hobby – or passion – is travelling.'

'It's quite an expensive hobby?'

'I couldn't afford to travel till I was 25. Then I inherited a modest property from an uncle. So I can now do a few trips each year.'

We had left Kerala and crossed the state border into Tamil Nadu.

'Incidentally,' continued Helmut, 'Cape Comorin was known as Kanya Kumari before the British occupied India, wasn't it?'

'Oh, yes,' I said. 'After all, it existed before the British came.'

'I know. It says in my guide-book that Ptolemy in the second century AD called it *Komaria Akroy* or something like that in Greek. And Marco Polo, who visited the place in the thirteenth century, described it as *Comori*. Both names have something to do with Kumari, a Sanskrit expression for the Virgin Goddess. Is it true that the Kumari Temple there is two thousand years old?'

Our conversation was cut short by a commotion at the front of the bus. Its cause, so it seemed, was a tall, powerfully built man who had got on the bus a few minutes earlier. His air of authority came not only from his large hypnotic eyes above his grey handlebar moustache, but also from his stentorian voice that reflected his official position.

He was an inspector, as I found out from one of my fellow passengers. Near him stood a medium-sized young man in khaki shirt and trousers. He was the bus conductor. He had been cocky, even arrogant. Now he was nervously fingering his leather pouch and looked thoroughly scared. It turned out that he had taken the fare from a passenger at Trivandrum, but not given him a ticket yet. The inspector was all for penalizing him: a fine of 10 rupees would have been enough to spoil his service record.

The driver, a wiry chap with a hatchet face, was pleading for the conductor. Both of them were natives of Kerala.

'But he committed the same offence the day before yesterday,' the inspector, a Tamil Nadu man, told him in English. 'My dear sir, you are nobody, I am nobody, but it is corrupt people like this gentleman here who have built palatial houses for themselves in big cities. At any rate, I have caught him red-handed again. He must understand that it is a state bus service and not his private company.'

'Forgive him, sir,' appealed the driver. 'He is new to the job; he does not yet know the rules of service. This will be a lesson to him. He won't do such a thing next time.'

'You deserve a bunch of roses for what you have said,' the inspector remarked, 'but I have my duty to perform.'

An old woman called out:

'Do give him a chance, inspector. Anybody can make a mistake. Have pity on him.'

Several other people joined in the plea for mercy.

The inspector, who was beginning to soften a little, put up his hand and asked for silence.

'Has anyone else a complaint against this person?' he then shouted.

In reply, some people shook their heads, while others murmured: 'No – no complaint.'

'Well, in that case . . .' came from the inspector as he was turning in the opposite direction.

Suddenly a finger shot up into the air.

'Here!' Helmut was saying aloud. 'I have a complaint to make.'

The other swung round:

'Really? Go on, I am listening.'

'He sold me the ticket but didn't give the change owing to me, saying he had none,' Helmut reported.

'What was the amount involved?'

'A trifle – only 10 paise. I don't mind the money, but I don't like to be cheated.'

'Ah, this is serious!' The inspector turned to the conductor, who mumbled something by way of explanation. 'May I have your name and address, please?'

Helmut took out a card and passed it on to him.

The inspector looked at it in a puzzled sort of way, as if he could not make it out. 'What nationality are you?'

'German. Helmut Hühnerfuss is my name.' Hühnerfuss means chickenfoot; I repressed a smile. The inspector gave the card another look before slipping it into his brief-case.

'Well,' he told the conductor, 'you certainly are making India popular among foreigners.'

By now almost everybody was trying to placate him, so he let the culprit off with a final warning. A moment later the conductor came up to Helmut. His manner, as he handed back the amount, was rigidly formal, thinly masking his shaken confidence.

'You really want him to lose his job?' asked the driver when we arrived in Kanya Kumari.

'No hard feelings,' replied Helmut as he shouldered his rucksack.

Leaving the bus station, we paused on a small rise by the road. From there you had a clear view of the headland and the sea beyond. Helmut consulted a pocket map he had unfolded.

'So here ends a continent,' he remarked. 'Exactly on this spot the eastern and western coastlines converge.'

He drew a camera from his pocket, a Kodak Instamatic, and started taking pictures. Then we pushed ahead. The stone-paved street rang with the recorded music issuing from loudspeakers in the crowded wayside stalls. I stopped at a juice bar. Helmut disappeared, saying he would see me in a minute.

When he got back, he asked whether the pineapple juice I was having was any good. I said it was all right, though there was a lot of ice in it. He did not care for iced drinks; they were bad for his throat. He had looked around and formed an opinion of the town. It was 'interesting but not fascinating'. There was a regular ferry service to a nearby rock memorial, but it was now closed till two in the afternoon, so he suggested having a bite to eat.

We popped into a restaurant. I mentioned that it was a vegetarian place.

'So much the better – vegetarian food is good as well as cheap,' he commented, going through the English section of the menu.

When he had placed his order with the waiter, he wanted to know about the dish, confessing he had no idea what it was.

'Why did you order it, in that case?' I asked.

'Because it was the cheapest,' was his reply.

I started off saying that the *dosa*, a typical South Indian dish, was a savoury pancake made from ground lentils and rice and eaten with sweet or sour chutney. Suddenly he got up. He had to see to something and would not be long. On the table he left his share of the bill. He turned up a quarter of an hour later. His food was cold, but he ate it quickly, declaring that it was crisp and delicious. Then he told me that his bus was leaving in half an hour.

'Going already?' I said. 'We've only just arrived.'

'Yes, but there's nothing special here.' He wiped his mouth with a paper handkerchief. 'So I'm off to Madurai. The bus will connect me with a steamer tonight. By tomorrow I'll be in that city famous for its sixteenth-century temples and many palaces, a city which was the capital of the Pandya dynasty from the fifth century BC to the fourteenth century AD.'

My face must have betrayed amusement or surprise, because Helmut Hühnerfuss found it necessary to add:

'I have a trained eye that sees things at a glance. My first impressions are never wrong. And life is short, but the world is endless. One must make the most of one's time.'

He shifted the rucksack to his back, said goodbye with a jerky wave of his hand and dashed out.

Shortly afterwards I left the restaurant, which stood at a fork in the street. I turned left. The sky was blue and a white sun warmed the cobble-stones. There were little shops in the narrow, sloping street. It was not long before I came to the temple of Kanya Kumari at the very tip of the cape. It had a white porch for an entrance, which was guarded by a lean old monk in a saffron robe.

Barring my way with his arm, he indicated a small enclosure against one of the porch's walls, where a young man was collecting money from some men who had just put their shoes or sandals in his care. I murmured an apology, instantly remembering that a Hindu or Muslim holy place can only be entered barefoot.

I was struck by what I next saw. The men who had left their shoes in the enclosure took off their shirts and their vests too before coming up to the monk, who nodded for them to pass.

'Is that because of the heat?' I asked him, pointing to the men's uncovered torsos.

The other shook his close-shaven head.

'Naked to the waist,' he said in a dry, grating voice, 'that's how people go into the temple. Naked to the waist.'

'But what's the reason?'

'It's one of our rules.'

A fully dressed woman, with an offering of flowers in her hands, came in barefoot from the street.

'What about her?' I asked as he let her go unchecked through the gate.

The monk made an irritable gesture, without replying.

'Why the naked-to-the-waist rule for men only?' I persisted.

'A rule is a rule,' he snapped out in reply.

'Thanks for the explanation.'

I went back into the street. After a while I walked into a bookshop. Behind a desk, to the left of the door, sat a dark middle-aged man. The aroma of freshly brewed coffee came from a cup in his right hand. I looked around. Most of the books were in Tamil, the principal language of over fifty million people in Tamil Nadu state and also spoken by about 20 per cent of the population of Sri Lanka.

'Can I help you?' the man asked me in English.

I mentioned what I wanted and he indicated a shelf with a cardboard box in which he kept picture postcards. I picked one up at random. It showed a bearded man in a turban, his cheeks puffed out, playing on a gourd-and-bamboo flute to a cobra with its hood sticking out of a cloth-lined basket.

'Has the south no snakes of its own?' I asked.

The other looked confused for an instant.

'Of course we have them,' he said. 'We have all kinds – more than you will find in the rest of India.'

'At any rate, you seem to be short of snake-charmers.'

'Why do you say that?'

'Because this card, as you can read on its back, is printed in New Delhi.'

'I get things from all over India for my customers.'

'Does that mean that you feel you're an Indian first and then a Tamil?'

'That is exactly how I feel. Those who feel otherwise aren't true patriots. Regionalism, no less than local patriotism, is the worst enemy of our national unity.' He smiled, adding: 'But I assure you that we have plenty of snakes in our state and no shortage of snake-charmers.'

'I haven't seen any snakes around so far, though.'

'You will find them in the countryside and sometimes in the rivers.'

'Are they poisonous, the water snakes?'

'River snakes are entirely harmless, but sea snakes are a 100 per cent poisonous.'

I certainly must have made a grimace, for he asked:

'Are you afraid of snakes?'

'Who isn't?'

A newspaper lay open on his desk. Pointing his thumb at it, he asked:

'Have you read of the Bengali?'

'At Calcutta zoo?' I said, taking in his reference to a widely reported event. 'Shut himself in with the deadliest of snakes for 75 days, didn't he?'

He nodded. 'The man has proved that snakes attack only when they are threatened.'

'But what about the sleeping people who fall victim to a snake-bite?'

'Oh, well, that's a puzzle,' he gracefully conceded.

I glanced at another card. The view on it was that of the offshore memorial to Swami Vivekananda (*swami*, Sanskrit for 'lord or 'master', is a title of respect for a Hindu religious teacher, who is often called a yogi).

'Curiously enough, there are only two sorts of cards in the box here,' I commented, having gone through the lot. 'Haven't you got any with a picture of the Kanya Kumari temple?'

The bookseller, who was lighting a cigarette, shook his head of shining black hair.

'In no other shop will you find even these,' he asserted. 'If you want something local, why not take the one with the rock memorial scene? It is quite beautiful. And besides – '

He broke off and gestured towards a smooth brown object that stood on the edge of his desk, which looked like a cigar case. On coming closer, I saw that it was a wooden slab, solid enough to serve as a paperweight. An Indian lotus was painted near its top. Below the flower ran a text in yellow English letters, which said:

'We have to learn yet that all religions, under whatever name they may be called, either Hindu, Buddhist, Muhammadan or Christian, have the same god, and he who derides any of these derides his own god.'

'Well?' he asked as if he expected a positive response.

Our glances met; I nodded.

'Swami Vivekananda, the author of these words, lived from 1863 to 1902,' he informed me weightily. 'He was a native of Bengal. Yet we in Tamil Nadu honoured him by building this monument in 1970 which must have cost millions. Why? Because he was a great man, an all-India figure. Both at home and abroad he taught the idea of a universal truth.'

Surrendering to his salesmanship, I bought some cards.

'Are you a local man?' I asked then.

'I was born in Kanya Kumari,' he replied. 'And I have lived here ever since.'

'Is this place no longer called Cape Comorin?'

'For us it has always been Kanya Kumari. Where does your good self come from?'

'I'm from Delhi.'

'Old Delhi or New Delhi?'

'I keep a foot in both. Ever been there?'

'No.' He shook his head apologetically. 'What business are you in, if I may ask?'

'It's to do with historical research.'

'History is my favourite subject.'

'I seem to be in luck then. It's my first visit to this town of yours. Could you explain something I noticed before coming to your shop, something I can't puzzle out?'

'I'll do my best,' he replied, bowing.

I told him about my encounter with the monk at the entrance to the temple.

'Hm,' he said and thought for a moment. 'Removing one's shoes is understandable, since they are unclean. But uncovering the upper part of one's body is a tradition. Originally it meant that you could not conceal weapons about your person; it was a precaution taken by the local rulers.'

'But weapons can be hidden in clothes worn below the waist too,' I objected. 'And they can easily be smuggled in by women, who are exempt from this requirement. You read of lady terrorists in the newspapers every day.'

'Those lady terrorists are all foreigners. Our Indian women are different. They only behave as terrorists towards their husbands.'

I complimented him on his wit.

'But the goddess in the temple is a virgin,' I went on. 'Is it proper for a man to pay her homage by stripping to the waist and showing off his biceps and pectoral muscles?'

He laughed, then said seriously:

'Baring one's chest is a sign of purity.'

Referring to the Badrinath Temple, a famous pilgrimage centre on the Tibetan border, far up in the Himalayas, I remarked:

'Such a sign of purity can give a man double pneumonia at this time of the year up there.'

'The practice differs from place to place in India,' he conceded, nodding. 'But this is how it is in the south. Things, however, are changing. Until recently, for example, the male pilgrims wishing to enter the inner temple here had to take off their trousers and put on a dhoti instead.'

'Yes, I saw a faded notice to that effect on a wall near the main entrance.'

'But now the temple is open to people of all races and religions,' he declared, not without a trace of pride in his voice.

'However, at the Birla Mandir, one of the best-known temples in Delhi, it is different,' I remarked. 'It was founded in 1939 by Mahatma Gandhi, who stood for communal harmony. And yet a notice there says that the temple is closed to the Muslims and Christians of Indian origin who live in India. It then goes on to ask the Muslims and Christians of foreign origin who live abroad to apply to a specially set-up reception office for a guided tour of the premises.'

'I see' – this coldly.

'Can you guess why?' I asked. 'Isn't it simply because tourists from industrial or oil-producing countries are supposed to be rich?'

The half-smoked cigarette dangled from the left-hand corner of his mouth. Judging by the preoccupied look on his face, something was troubling him. As he leaned forward a little, a shaft of sunshine from the door lit up the *tilak* mark on his forehead – a dab of red paste flecked with rice and saffron. I wondered whether in his case it was a sign of good luck, of devoutness or of a high caste. A cloud of smoke issued from behind the cigarette between his lips.

'Are you a Hindu?' he asked suddenly.

'Do you know that the word Hindu was coined by the Persians when they invaded north-west India in the sixth century BC?'

He regarded me oddly.

'Yes,' I continued, 'the Persians had trouble pronouncing the initial "s" of the Sindhu, which was what the Indus River was called. So they described the people of the Indus Valley as Hindu and their land as Hindustan – the suffix "stan" means "place" in Persian.'

'I didn't know that,' he admitted. 'But are you a Hindu?'

Something from history came into my mind. The Aryans, who came from the plains of Central Asia and swept across northern India about 2000 BC, belonged to an Indo-European family speaking Sanskrit, which is related to Greek, Latin and the Germanic and Slav languages. By the sixth century BC, they had conquered the rest of the subcontinent, including South India. The beliefs and customs of the subjugated Dravidians (the name given by the Aryans to the people living in Southern India) and other local people became, in the course of centuries, a part of the Aryan (in Sanskrit *Arya* means 'noble') or Hindu civilization.

In a light vein, therefore, I was about to ask if he wanted to know whether I was a Hindu by birth or by conviction. But he was watching me with growing mistrust. It seemed possible that he would not even believe me when I said I was a real Hindu. So I had to think of something better to say.

I cast about in my mind for inspiration. Thanks to the upbringing my parents gave me, I had a comprehensive knowledge of Hindu religion and mythology by the time I was of school age. My father was a doctor, who never insisted on my being religious. He was a man of erudition too. 'The Ganga (the Ganges) is flowing before you; drink your fill of its waters', was one of his sayings. By this he meant that all his learning was there for me to absorb. He had perfect mastery of Sanskrit. He knew Vedic Sanskrit, in which the great books of hymns, called the Veda, (literally, 'wisdom' or 'knowledge') were composed between the fifteenth and second century BC, as well as the later classical Sanskrit of India's sacred, philosophical and poetic literature. My instruction at home began with a Sanskrit grammar in verse, which I was required to learn by heart.

'Don't bother about the meaning at this stage,' my father said whenever I grumbled about not understanding the text. 'It will become clear once you've mastered the whole book.'

Somehow, I developed an inward resistance to these attempts at teaching me, perhaps because too much was expected of me. I tried consciously to forget all that had been drilled into me, and eventually I succeeded. Long afterwards, however, I was aware of a curious phenomenon: things from the early childhood recurred to me quite unexpectedly.

That was what happened then, in that shop. Of the four Vedas, the Rig-Veda is the oldest. Its golden text is a hymn dedicated to Savitri, a solar deity. I murmured the words that had come back to me. Their effect on the bookseller was dramatic. The look of suspicion suddenly left his oval, firm-fleshed face.

'The *Gayatri*!' he exclaimed, taking my hand in both of his and pressing it fervently.

'You know it?'

The question visibly surprised him.

'Which Hindu doesn't?' he replied. 'After all, it is the most holy verse in our scripture – I chant it first thing each morning. You must be a Brahman. Right?'

'How did you guess?'

'From the excellent Sanskrit in which you recited the *Gayatri* verse,' he explained triumphantly.

It was astonishing the way he had drawn his inference. Obviously he associated fluency in Sanskrit with someone from the caste traditionally regarded as being the source of priests and learned men – that was to say, with a Brahman. A likely explanation suggested itself to me. There are two main ethnic groups in India: Aryan in the North (72 per cent) and Dravidian in the South (25 per cent). The languages spoken by the Aryan group are Indo-European, descended from Sanskrit. And those spoken by the other group – like Tamil, Malayalam, Kannada and Telugu – belong to the Dravidian family of non–Indo-European languages; they were in use over most of India before it was stormed by the Aryans in the second millennium BC. Tamil, the bookseller's mother tongue, is known for its rich literature, dating back to the second century AD.

'Do you know Sanskrit?' I asked.

'A little,' he replied. 'But I have a good ear for it. After all, it is the sacred language of our religion. And, according to Article 345 of the Indian Constitution, it is one of the fifteen languages any state can adopt for official purposes. Anyway, we can talk freely now – about anything you like.'

'What sort of goddess is Kanya Kumari?'

'The Virgin is an incarnation of the great goddess Devi.'

And Devi, as I knew, is the consort of Shiva. She is often called his *shakti*, or female creative power. In her nature she mirrors the various activities of her husband, and shows herself consequently in forms that are either gentle or stern, each time under a different name.

'On this occasion,' the bookseller was saying, 'she was born as Kanya Kumari. She was the daughter of a nobleman or some royal person. She grew into such a beautiful young woman that Shiva fell in love with her and began following her everywhere. At last he couldn't control his passion any longer. One evening he approached her, looking desperate. She said she would marry him on one condition: that he bring her a coconut that has no eyes and a stick of sugar-cane that has no joints, before the cock crowed the following morning. After a long search he found these. But just as he was about to give them to her, along came that divine mischief-maker, Narada, who at once changed himself into a raven and imitated a cock-crow. And so it happened that Shiva, thinking he had not managed things in time, left in disappointment.'

'What was Kanya Kumari's reaction?' I asked.

'One of relief.'

'She didn't like Shiva?'

'She did. But she had come down to earth to destroy a demon king. She could only do that job if she were a virgin. This town is said to be the site of the battle in which she killed him.'

'Can one believe that all these stories actually happened?'

'On the face of it, it's a silly story,' he admitted. 'Shiva, being all-powerful, could have got the eye-less coconut and the joint-less sugar-cane just by wishing. And he could easily have told the difference between the cry of a raven and that of a cock. But, like most legends, this one means something. It shows, for example, that even the gods cannot always win, as they too are ruled by a higher authority. And then, it stresses the ideal of duty. The legend teaches that one shouldn't let anything stand in the way of one's duty – like the virgin who turned down

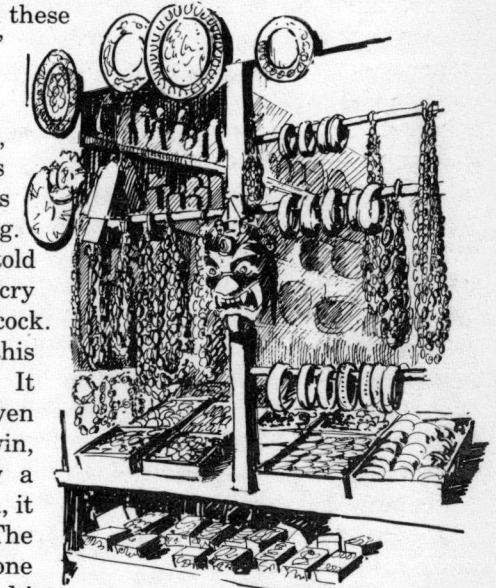

the love of a mighty god like Shiva for the sake of her mission.'

I made a leisurely tour of the town. It seemed to be market day and the bazaar I was in, crowded with shoppers and tourists. I walked between the long, narrow rows of little booths selling images of the goddess worshipped here, as well as ornamental objects made from wood, metal, papier mâché, shells and beads. I did not miss seeing the Mahatma Gandhi Memorial either, an imposing white building of bold design, extending from the shore into the sea.

It was with some surprise that I realized that I was once again outside the Kanya Kumari Temple. I resolved to get in this time. Depositing my sandals with the shoe attendant, I stripped to the waist and headed for the entrance. A fattish man in khaki shirt and shorts had replaced the monk as sentry. He asked to see the cloth bag hanging from my shoulder.

'You can't go in,' he then declared.

'Why not?'

'You have a camera in your bag. No camera allowed.'

'I won't take pictures,' I told him.

He shook his head. 'You must leave it outside.'

'Look here, the film in it is all used up. It has no exposures left.'

He shook his head with greater emphasis.

'Very well, I'll take the film out,' I said. 'Will it be all right then?'

' "No camera," I said.'

'What should I do with it? Can I leave it somewhere here?'

'No camera!'

'But why not, when it's empty? They don't mind such things in other temples.'

With an imperious wave of his hand, he dismissed me. He looked so self-important that it was all I could do not to laugh.

The signboard over a single-storeyed office on the shore read THE VIVEKANANDA SOCIETY. This charitable organization, named after the famous Swami, runs the ferry service as well as arranging accommodation and some minor facilities for tourists and pilgrims. Several people stood about. Half the office veranda was flooded with the afternoon sun. In the shady other half reigned a bearded man of thirty-odd years. On the table before him lay a roll of tickets, a register and some papers. I told him I wanted to make a trip to the rock memorial.

His brownish eyes threw me an indifferent glance.

'Tomorrow,' he said through his projecting teeth that seemed to make his dark face still longer.

'Why not today?' I asked.

He pointed at his watch: it showed three minutes past five.

'Sorry, I didn't know you closed at five,' I said. 'Won't you give me the customary five minutes' grace?'

Silently he gathered up the papers from his table.

'There's a ferry-boat waiting to leave – I've just seen it at the pier,' I said. 'It's only half full. There's plenty of room on it. Do please give me a ticket.'

He did not look at me. 'Tomorrow,' he repeated.

'But I can't stay here till then. I must return to Delhi this very evening.'

'Tomorrow,' he declared.

'It's my first visit to your town and I may never come here again,' I said, injecting a note of despair into my voice.

'Tomorrow,' he echoed.

'Can't you really do me the favour?'

'Tomorrow.'

'Please! Can't I soften your heart at all?'

'Tomorrow – tomorrow – tomorrow.' And he picked up his papers and walked away.

I stepped off the veranda. In the distance, where the Indian Ocean and the Arabian Sea meet, soared the temple-domed memorial to Swami Vivekananda. The saffron colour of the memorial stood out in sharp contrast to the deep blue of the sea and the clear blue of the sky. The two rocks supporting the monument are called Pitru and Matra. I had heard that the pilgrimage rites included bathing there. I wondered whether a ritual dip at that sacred spot would not have washed away my past sins, leaving me free to commit new ones of a lighter and more delightful nature.

The Turning-Point

I left Kottayam on a clear, sunny day the following week. I had no idea then of the predicament I was shortly going to find myself in. So it was in a cheerful mood that I got off the bus in Trivandrum. The railway station hummed with activity. I could see the nearest platform flashing in the midday sun. Suddenly a shadow swept along it: the express to Delhi had pulled in.

People stood about the booking-offices in thick clusters. Like them, I was waiting for the list of passengers to be posted up. Its appearance caused a general stir. Those who found their names on it hurried off with their luggage towards the train at the platform. I went over the list for what must have been the fifth time. But my name just was not there, which meant that I was stuck, that I could not return to Delhi.

It seemed downright crazy, impossible. An oversight, I decided, was responsible for my name having been missed out from the list. I had to see someone about it. The white lettering over a door said: Assistant Station Master. I went in. The official I came upon was a dark slender man who heard me out quietly but without interest. Only once did he stop chewing his betel leaf, and that was to tell me he did not deal with such cases.

Next I approached the inspector of tickets and reservations. Though not perhaps quite 40, he was already grey-haired. I had hardly begun speaking when he made a sign for me to wait. He appeared to be hunting for something among the papers on his desk. A pair of braces held up trousers over a stomach that bulged out like a football. Then he struck his forehead with his fist and said aloud: 'Oh, rubbish!' A jacket was draped over the back of his chair. He dived into its left-hand pocket and brought out the handkerchief he had doubtless been so intently searching for. It was crumpled and dirty. Almost the whole of his face disappeared into it. Then he blew his nose for a full minute and cleared his throat most thoroughly. At last he looked up with his bloodshot eyes and asked what he could do for my excellency. I told him. He opened a folder and checked a list of passengers.

'Sorry,' he said with a slow shake of his head, 'but your name is not here.'

'That's rather strange,' I retorted. 'A week ago – on the seventh of this month, to be exact – I was at your Divisional Office. The reservation supervisor assured me that I'd have a reserved seat on the KK Express today.'

He frowned in thought.

'Hold on,' he said, reaching for another folder. He scrutinized some more lists.

'No,' he spoke with finality, 'you have no reservation on any of the trains going to Delhi this week.'

'But the supervisor promised!'

'I believe you,' he nodded, 'but that gentleman has not kept his promise. So I am unable to help you.'

'I'm in a desperate plight,' I groaned. 'I can't stay here; I have to get back to Delhi at the earliest. Could you give me a tip what to do?'

'Go to Madras,' he said without a moment's reflection. 'You will get a seat there.'

'Madras!' I exclaimed in astonishment. 'Are you serious?'

'Why do you think I am not serious?'

'But Madras is such a long way off.'

'What do you mean? Leave today and you will be there tomorrow evening.'

'And if I don't get a reservation in Madras either?'

A flush rose to his flabby cheeks.

'Why did you ask me for advice when you didn't mean to act on it?' he nearly shouted.

'Of course I'll act on it,' I said to soothe him. 'That was very kind of you.'

It soon became evident, however, that I had no choice but to follow his advice. When I was in Trivandrum the previous week, I had bought a second-class ticket for my return journey. I got it cancelled and the fare refunded; then I bought a new ticket, so that now I had a booking to Madras, where I would have to apply for one to Delhi.

That settled, I consoled myself with the thought that the impending trip need not turn out to be a bad thing after all. And since I had to be in Madras anyway, I might just as well stay there for a bit.

Meanwhile I was at a loose end, as my train did not leave for a few hours. How about a dash to the zoo or museum? The idea appealed to me. I hired a rickshaw. As it set off, I began thinking about my friend Varghese. The previous day I had gone to say goodbye to him at the hospital in Kottayam. He had not yet recovered from the operation, but he assured me of feeling almost fit. We were reminiscing about our days in London.

'You used to roll in money then,' I bantered. 'Don't you miss those times?'

'I really do,' he replied, smiling. 'But my roots are here. Mind you, it took me quite a while to adjust to the Indian conditions again. I've reconciled myself to my modest income now. My ideals too I have retained. And I've done a few things. Have delivered more than one paper. And I've a couple of books to my credit.'

'Indeed? Congratulations, old chap! What are the books about?'

'Oh, my subject – socioeconomic stuff, you know. I also edit *State and Society*, a quarterly journal published by our Institute.'

I wished him luck with his plans and asked if he enjoyed being at the Indian Institute for Regional Development Studies.

'On the whole,' he said, 'I do. Would you believe it, I'm one of its founder-members. For the first two years I was only paid a nominal salary. The Institute is fully established now. It gets a grant from the state government and has links with major scientific bodies in India. By the way, we're starting on the residential building in two weeks. You'll stay on the campus when next you come.'

'Shall I see you in Europe one of these days?'

As if he were letting me into a secret, he whispered:

'Yes, in a few months' time.'

'Oh, really?'

He grinned:

'The University of Amsterdam wants me for a three-month editorial job on a research project they recently completed in Kerala . . .'

The rickshaw pulled up with a jerk, interrupting my train of thought. I looked up and saw the trim figure of a policeman on point duty. Wearing a khaki uniform with a pith helmet, he stood on a circular stone platform, protected from the sun by a wooden canopy shaped like an umbrella. In one hand he held a metal disc on which the letters STOP were painted a bright red; it was pointed in our direction.

'How much further?' I asked the rickshaw driver, who replied with a gesture implying that we were close to our destination.

Suddenly the policeman withdrew the STOP sign. There was a thick short iron bar in his other hand which he clanged against the metal rod supporting the canopy above him. It was the signal for the traffic to proceed. The rickshaw shot forward, entering a wide street. We drove past the red brick structure of Kerala University and the Gothic façade of a church. Leaving the city's recently built stadium on our left, we turned down an avenue. It led to the museum, the grey green of whose gable roofs stood out against the pale blue of the afternoon sky. I climbed out of the rickshaw at the entrance to the zoo next door.

Two or three hours afterwards, I was strolling through the outer court of the museum towards the main entrance. Two upright shapes, coal-black and petrified in appearance, loomed at the side of the gravelled path. A notice was attached to the low rail fence. I read:

FOSSILIZED TRUNKS OF TREES
TWENTY MILLION YEARS OLD
FROM THE NATIONAL FOSSIL PARK
TIRNOVAKKARI SOUTH ARCOT DISTRICT TAMIL NADU

As I contemplated, the two shapes, I became conscious of steps behind me. They drew nearer and stopped. A man in spotless white was standing beside me. He was about 60 and completely bald. The eyes that looked out of his gentle, handsome features were penetrating.

'The sun is strong and you are bareheaded,' he remarked in English.

I thanked him for the shelter he offered me under his umbrella.

'Have you done both the zoo and the museum?' he asked.

'I just hurried through. Didn't have much time.'

'Were you impressed by anything in particular?'

In the sculpture department I had noticed three white seals. They were from Mohenjo-Daro, the site of the Indus civilization that flourished about the third millennium BC. What I had found admirable was the delicate workmanship of the patterns engraved on each of the seals: a man between two tigers, a man under a pipal tree, and a unicorn.

I spoke of them, adding:

'They looked so fresh as to seem modern.'

The other pursed his lips, frowning, then smiled.

'Perhaps they *are* modern,' he said.

'It says there that they date from 2500 BC.'

'Yes, but we mustn't accept everything we are told,' he said in a patient tone of voice. 'Do you know about the Piltdown Man? In 1912 someone came upon a skull, a jaw and a canine tooth at a place called Piltdown, in England. He put the skull together again and sold it to the British Museum in London. It belonged, so he claimed, to a type of man that lived five hundred thousand years ago, having an ape's jaw but a completely modern head. That upset all the theories of evolution known up to that time. It was only some forty years later – in 1953, to be precise – that tests proved the skull to be 100 per cent fake. So there you are!'

'You have a point there.'

'They are not above placing bits of ordinary glass in a museum

show-case and declaring them to be so many centuries or millennia old.
You know why?'

I said I did not.

'Because they are sure that people will believe them,' he explained.
'Take yourself, for example. You are standing in front of these fossil
trees. Didn't you stop here because you were lured by that notice which
says they are twenty million years old?'

'You seem to be a good judge of people.'

'Hm,' he said as if he had not heard me. 'Twenty million years! The
thing is beyond one's wildest imagination. Now, if I were to get twenty
million rupees, I would never succeed in counting them – not even in
twenty years. Incidentally, were you at the monkey house?'

'Just had a quick look.'

'There's a large ferocious-looking baboon there – a mandrill. It has a
violet bottom ringed with scarlet and a clown-like face marked with
red and blue stripes. A notice on its cage states that this animal is of *a
kind seen in a nightmare.*'

'I do remember seeing that,' I put in.

'Now, I have nightmares at least five times a week. But never have I
seen such a creature in any of my bad dreams. Have you, by any
chance?'

'I don't think so.'

'Well, you understand what I'm driving at? This is an age of experts,
of specialists. They are supposed to know better than we do; they do our
thinking for us and tell us how to run our lives. But we must not let
ourselves be taken in; we must always be on our guard against them.
I'll give another illustration of the disinformation they spread. Did you
visit the Reptile House?'

'No, I had to give it a miss.'

'Well, a printed notice there tells you how to cure a snake-bite. Tie a
bandage above the bite, it says, and make a quarter-inch-long and a
quarter-inch-deep incision on the fang wound. Then suck out the blood
and lymph by mouth (if you have no cuts) or by mechanical means.
After that, apply a salt-water dressing. And finally take some anti-
snake serum intravenously.

'Now all that is well meant, but confused, confusing and dangerous.
First aid can do tremendous harm unless it is given skilfully, and it is of
no earthly use once the poison has spread. One of the important things,
for instance, is to drink no alcohol; yet there's not a word about it on the
notice.'

'Are you a doctor?'

'No, I'm not, but my brother is one,' he replied. 'I am a retired
lecturer in philosophy. He – that is my brother – has treated hundreds

of snake-bite cases successfully. A polyvalent serum is the most effective antidote to the poison of all local snakes. It should be sold cheap and be available at every chemist's . . .'

He continued to hold his umbrella over my head as he accompanied me to the bus stop.

'Keep up the good work,' I said to him. 'The world needs reformers like you.'

'But how much can one man achieve?' he wanted to know.

'A great deal. There's a saying in the Punjab: even a single Sikh, wherever he be, is like an army 125,000 strong.'

A smile illuminated his entire face. The bus to the railway station had come and moved off as I got in. I looked back. The philosopher was still waving to me from the street.

The train drew out of Trivandrum at 16.50. I had a seat opposite a young man. The hair at the back of his neck was arranged in a series of waves. His long, smooth face with its aquiline nose was bent over a newspaper in which he seemed to be engrossed. After a while, he folded the paper and started fanning himself with it, even though the carriage window was open and gusts of wind were blowing in. Our eyes happened to meet and we exchanged a smile. Pointing to the newspaper in his hand, I asked conversationally:

'How do you like the *Hindu*?'

'The best of the national dailies,' he replied with emphasis. 'For years I've been keeping its Sunday magazine supplements. The amount of general knowledge they contain is terrific.'

'I too used to collect the weekly supplements of the *Statesman*. I could never get round to reading them. Later I sold them as waste paper – by the kilo.'

'Not me; I could never do such a thing to the *Hindu*. Just now I'm working as a trainee, but I'll be a fully-fledged chartered accountant next summer. I'll have a lot more time then. Where, by the way, are you going?'

'Now to Madras and from there to Delhi.'

'So you'll change at Quilon. You will have to cool your heels for hours before your connection with the Madras Mail.'

'Yes,' I said resignedly. 'It's a long wait. Are you from these parts?'

He nodded. 'I work in Trivandrum but live in Quilon, which is my hometown.'

'What sort of a place is Quilon?'

'Well, it is a big commercial city,' he told me. 'And as a seaport it has quite a history. In olden times it had dealings with the Persians, Arabs, Greeks and Romans. Marco Polo, the Italian globe-trotter of the thirteenth century, called it Coilum in his books. The Portuguese were the first European traders to land here. They were followed by the Dutch in 1662. And the Dutch were followed by the English. Yes, and today – today there are three colleges in the city. And perhaps you know that the cashew nuts of Quilon are famous all over the world.'

'They sell cheaply, I hope, at least locally.'

'Cheap?' A scowl pulled at the corners of his sensual mouth. 'Not for my pocket at least. Nothing is cheap these days, except the words of our politicians. You live in Delhi?'

'From time to time. Ever been there?'

'It is too far for us people here. I couldn't afford the train fare.'

'But you have some idea of Delhi no doubt?'

'Very little – in fact none.'

'You must have heard about the Red Fort.'

He shook his head. 'Nope.'

'I mean, the historic Red Fort – from whose ramparts the Prime Minister delivers the Republic Day address every year.'

'Never heard of it.'

'It's hard to believe it of an educated newpaper-reader like you,' I said, softening my remark with a smile.

'I don't know anything about the North, just as you perhaps don't know much about the South,' he said without anger. 'So we are quits.'

We reached Quilon at 18.30. The Madras Mail was due to leave at 22.50. Somehow I had to kill time; what better way of doing that than exploring the town a bit. From the station I wandered down a street that seemed to go on and on. I became conscious of the heat and my parched throat the moment I caught sight of a shop sign announcing the sale of alcoholic drinks. I bought a bottle of beer. Could I drink it on the spot?

'You can,' answered the shopkeeper with a merry twinkle in his eyes, 'provided you have friends among the local police.'

'Unfortunately, I haven't had the opportunity to make friends with those gentlemen yet, as I landed here only a little while ago.'

'Never mind then.' He laughed. 'If a policeman spots you, you can get out of trouble by ordering a bottle for him too.'

I drank my beer. 'Could you explain something? On the way from the station to your place I must have asked at least ten tobacconists, but they had only one brand of cigarettes on sale – the Panama – which I don't smoke. And these they sold loose, not in packets.'

'What is your favourite brand?'

I told him.

'Well, I can oblige you' – he giggled – 'because we have the same taste.' He offered me one from his packet and even lit it for me.

'Thanks,' I said. 'But why this cigarette famine in your town?'

'It's the fourteenth of February today.'

'Has that any bearing on the crisis?'

'It's Shivaratri today, don't you know?' This was a reference to the Hindu festival in honour of Shiva, who is worshipped with flowers during the night.

'True, but I fail to see the connection all the same.'

'Lord Shiva doesn't smoke, so no cigarettes today. But I am a Christian. And your good self?'

'I'm something of everything.'

The temple I later dropped into was bright with oil lamps. Bare-footed worshippers, including people who seemed poor, were making their offerings of fruit, flowers and money. I was touched by the expression of devotion and humility on their faces. Yet, curiously, none of the images of Shiva about the place inspired me the way they used to when I was a boy. In those old days I often saw a vision in which God appeared to me in his different human incarnations, and I was known in the neighbourhood as one who enjoyed spiritual grace. At present, however, it was only the tune of the songs and the music in the temple that stirred me.

Back in the railway station, I stopped at a tea-and-coffee stall. A thin, long-haired man next to me was eating a snack off a banana leaf. The assistant behind the counter, a young chap with a few wisps of hair on his chin, asked me in broken English:

'Your home, please?'

'Delhi,' I replied, adding: 'One tea – very strong.'

The man beside me paused in his eating.

'Oh, you are from Delhi?' he asked with sudden interest.

'That's right.'

'But why all by yourself?'

'Well, you know, that's how it sometimes is.'

He said something to the assistant in Malayalam and then turned to me:

'I am the proprietor of the stall. I would like to serve you personally.'

He dropped the empty banana leaf into a bin and was on the other side of the counter the next minute. The inner walls of the stall were hung with portraits. I pointed to one that showed a youth with three horizontal lines of sandalwood paste on his forehead, carrying a trident.

'Who is that?' I asked.

'It is Subrahmanya, the war god, as a boy,' the stall-keeper answered. 'You in the North probably call him Karttikeya.'

He went on to explain two other pictures, whose subjects I did not tell him I knew: Ganapati, the elephant-headed god of fortune and learning; and Sarasvati, the goddess of the creative arts, with a four-stringed musical instrument called a *vina*.

Then he indicated the rest of the portraits representing the saintly Vivekananda, the philosopher Radhakrishnan, and national leaders like Mahatma Gandhi and Nehru.

I took a sip of the tea he had handed me with a graceful bow.

'Good?' he asked.

'Yes,' I said. 'First class.'

We got to chatting about this and that.

'How much?' I asked, putting my empty cup down on the counter.

'You pay nothing,' he replied.

'But I must. I did enjoy the tea after all.'

'It is on me.'

'But you don't know me.'

'You seem to be a nice man. Isn't that enough?'

'Still, it's too much. Do please let me pay.'

He shook his head firmly:

'In no case.'

I returned the money I had taken out of my wallet.

'It's been a pleasure being your guest. Tell me, what makes you so kind to someone you have never seen before?'

'Me kind? Oh, no!' He gave a modest smile. 'It is just that I fast every Tuesday. Fasting, as you know, is good for the soul and for the body too. It is a method of telling the body that I am its master and not the other way round.'

'And it makes you generous too?'

'The matter is quite simple. What to do with the money I save on my food on the fast day? It won't be moral to spend it on myself. So I use it like this: I give free tea or coffee to a different man every day.'

'To your friends as well?'

'Never,' he declared. 'That would mean impressing them with my goodness; that would be like doing something for profit, direct or indirect. And only an action that is selfless can be virtuous. For this reason I offer a cup of tea to a total stranger, whenever that is possible.'

*　　*　　*

It was a warm night. Even the overhead fan did not seem to cool the compartment, which was bathed in the light of a powerful bulb in the ceiling. The train had been in motion for about an hour. I had just finished a game of cards with two Punjabis seated beside me: Handa, a stocky young man with regular features and curly hair; and Suri, a lean, good-humoured Sikh business man with a dyed beard. On the bunk opposite was Mummy, a big-boned woman with dimpled cheeks and rich-blonde hair. She wore a skirt and a jacket, with a tiny gold cross suspended from a gold chain round her neck, at the breast of her white blouse. On her lap she had a novel, entitled *Jane's Last Chance*: it was published by a London firm specializing in romantic fiction. Next to her sat a red-headed and red-bearded giant of a man with a large yellow metal ring in one nostril. He was absorbed in a book open at a page covered with diagrams, and the look on his face warned us against disturbing him. On the bunk above him and Mummy lay a sharp-featured, tough-looking young chap, his moustache curled up at the ends. From time to time he shot a calculating glance at Mummy below.

When Handa had mentioned the city in Punjab he came from, I could not help exclaiming:

'Jullundur! Oh, really?'

'Do you know Jullundur?' he asked.

'Know it? I taught three years in the DAV College there.'

He inclined his head in a bow.

'I have as much respect for a teacher as I have for my parents,' he then said. 'You know, I've never seen my parents holding hands or kissing or seated on the same bed. Their way of living has been a good example to me. My elder brother too is a copy of my father. He works in the publicity department of Jai Shree Pictures. This company makes films that make you think. I saw one recently.'

He outlined the plot: the erring husband returns to his faithful wife, leaving the beautiful but selfish woman who had bewitched him, who was, in fact, only interested in his money.

'I saw it three times, and each time I wept,' he concluded. 'I took my wife along too – we were married two years ago. It's a film you can show the whole family without once lowering your eyes in shame.'

I learned that he was a mechanic in a firm that made locomotives.

'After my matric, I applied for a job there,' he told me. 'The manager, who interviewed me, wanted to test my common sense. He began by telling a story. One morning a night watchman went to his employer, a big business man, and said: "Sir, I had a bad dream last night. Don't go to Delhi by the Punjab Mail tomorrow. The train will have an accident and you will be killed." The business man thought about it and postponed the journey he was to make. Next day the train did meet with an accident, and many lives were lost. So the business man called the night watchman. He gave him a reward of 10,000 rupees and then dismissed him from service. Now, the manager asked me: "Why was the man dismissed?" '

Turning to those of us who had been listening to him, Handa said:

'Does anybody know?'

Silence was followed by murmurs:

'No. Why was he dismissed?'

'Because he was sleeping when he should have been guarding his boss's property,' replied Handa. 'He got the reward, however, for telling the business man his dream and saving his life.'

'Was that what you told your manager?' asked Mummy.

'Yes,' said Handa. 'And he was so pleased that he gave me the job.'

'Well done!' She applauded.

'After joining,' Handa was saying, 'I got to know a fitter there. He was so wise and experienced that everyone called him Ustad, which means "master". He taught me two principles of life. Number one, never desire another man's wife. And number two, never live for just yourself. Why? Because the world is a caravanserai. Ustad told me a little story. A maharaja was coming out of his palace one day when he ran into a yogi, who asked him: "Whose serai is this?" His highness was offended. "A serai?" he said angrily. "Why, my good man, this is a famous palace named after the great and mighty Bahadur Singh.' The yogi asked: "Who was Bahadur Singh?" The maharaja said: "My father." The yogi asked: "Who lived here before him?" The maharaja said: "His father." The yogi asked: "And before him?" The maharaja replied: "His father's father and so on – my ancestors." At this the yogi said: "A lot of people have been staying here. And after you die your son and his son and his son's son and their descendants will stop here for a while and then vanish. So isn't this palace of yours, like the world, a caravanserai?" '

Handa had earlier remarked that he did not like speaking English, since it was the language of the former British rulers of India, but that he was forced to use it in South India to communicate with the local people. Hindi expressions often crept into his speech. Mummy understood some Hindi, though she pronounced it badly. In reply to Handa's question, she had said that she had five sons and two daughters. All of them were graduates and had good jobs.

'Mummy is Anglo-Indian,' Handa told me then.

I looked at her and she nodded, smiling.

'I went to a school that had an Anglo-Indian headmaster,' I told her.

'How nice! I hope you were happy there.'

'Oh yes, quite happy.'

That, however, was not strictly true. My father had put me in that school because English was taught there at an earlier stage than in the other local schools, and a good knowledge of English was supposed to get you a job easily.

It was a longish walk from our house and I had trouble being in time for assembly, held at seven each morning in an open space behind the school wall that commanded a view of the only gate. I was late at least twice a week. I was not an exception, though, because there were always other similar culprits with me. We stood aside in a line intended for latecomers, waiting for Mr Frank, the headmaster, to punish us for our offence.

There, in front of the whole school, he loomed in his customary suit of white silk that set off the blue-black dye of his clipped moustache. A plump man of medium height, Mr Frank was flanked as usual by the assistant headmaster and the school secretary; the rest of the staff were stationed near their classes, seeing to it that the pupils behaved themselves. The assembly followed a set procedure. Mr Frank began by reading something from the Bible, discussing it and ending with a message of love and forgiveness. Next came the official announcements. These were followed by a song in praise of God, sung by all present. Then the school was dismissed.

Immediately afterwards, Mr Frank walked with measured steps towards the line of scared latecomers. He raised one arm high up in the air. If you drew back your hand before his cane touched it, the punishment was doubled. And it was trebled if you did it again. The strokes from his cane left welts in the palm that ached for the rest of the day.

Sometimes I went to the school to watch a football match late in the afternoon. Mr Frank lived on the school premises; next to his house was a tennis court where he could be seen having a game with his friends, who were Anglo-Indians. Occasionally I saw his daughter Stella there. She was a healthy and not unattractive young woman with bobbed hair, who wore Western-style clothes. Her brother Robin often played against her. He was a squat, pug-nosed boy, nearly 18, with a cocky air.

None of them were said to mix with Indians, though the school contained only Indian pupils. The Anglo-Indians were a tightly knit and self-contained community. Their children went to special schools that emphasized the English language and culture as well as distinctive group customs and manners; they only attended church services in English and joined segregated clubs. As a result, Anglo-Indians developed into a sort of caste. They looked down on Indians. At the same time they imitated and looked up to the British, who rejected them socially, though allowing them certain privileges. During the struggle for Independence, most of them stuck up for British rule, earning the mistrust and disapproval of numerous Indians.

The Constitution defines an Anglo-Indian as 'a person whose father or any of whose other male progenitors in the male line is or was of

European descent but who is domiciled within India or is born within such territory of parents habitually resident therein and not established for temporary purposes only'.

Most of the mixed marriages from which Anglo-Indian children were born took place before the twentieth century. These were between low-ranking British army or civilian men and Hindu or Muslim women at the lower end of the social scale. The concessions the Anglo-Indians enjoy at present include a quota of seats in the national parliament and in a few state parliaments. Some of them have reached top positions in business, in the army and in the air force. The majority of them, however, are employed in the railway and postal services.

'Do you feel yourself to be Indian or English?' Handa had asked Mummy.

'Neither the Indians nor the English seem to like us,' she replied after a moment's thought. 'So I don't know where I stand.'

Her reply reminded me of something an Indologist had told me in Berlin the previous year. A woman he had met at a cultural function in Delhi asked him:

'Don't you dislike me?'

'Why should I dislike you?' he wondered.

'I'm an Anglo-Indian, you know.'

'That makes no difference to me,' he remarked. 'I'm not English. I'm a European, a German.'

Handa was saying to Mummy:

'Each man sees the world as it is reflected in the mirror of his mind; he judges it according to his own nature. A holy man who had renounced the world – a *sannyasi*, that is – was bathing in a river at five in the morning. He saw another man bathing on the opposite bank and thought: "What a good fellow! He is washing himself so early because he wants to meditate and pray." The other man was a thief. When he saw the *sannyasi* he thought: "What a smart fellow! He is washing himself so early because he wants to commit a theft while his victims are still in bed."

'That is how things are, Mummy. Take Nathuram Godse, the man who killed Mahatma Gandhi. When Gandhi saw him he took him for a nice boy who had come to attend the prayer meeting. But Godse took Gandhi for a bad man who was robbing Hindus to help Muslims. So he shot him. As he lay dying Gandhi, spoke the name of God; then, referring to his murderer, he said: "Forgive him." So we should not bother about who likes us and who does not like us. The world is full of all types of people: some are mean, some are noble. I, for one, like you. And I'm sure that all of us here like you.'

'Thank you,' said the woman. 'You're very kind indeed. Life, however, is full of strains and stresses and problems, especially when one has a large family as I have. Anyway, I'm going to Australia next month. That ought to do me good.'

'Going for ever?' asked Handa.

'Dear me, no. Just to visit my youngest son in Sydney. He is a commercial artist.'

'Art is like the ocean,' remarked Handa. 'The deeper you dive, the better the pearls you find.'

'Do you paint in your spare time?' asked Mummy.

'No, but I don't want to sell my art. When I was younger I used to act the part of Sita in the Ramlila shows.' He was speaking of the theatrical plays, based on the epic *Ramayana*, about the life of Rama and his wife Sita. 'Now that I have become a bit fuller, I only play the role of Rama. But I've never taken money for my parts, though the other actors get paid for theirs. Sometime ago I wrote a novel which I called *The Birthday Present*. It is the story of a landless labourer. One day he goes to the rich landowner he works for. He tells him that his son is critically ill and that he needs money for the boy's treatment. He gets a "no" for an answer. Result: the son dies. The father then kills the landowner in a fit of anger. He is sent to prison for life. Every year he saves his prison allowance to buy a birthday present for his dead son.'

'Wonderful,' said Mummy. 'Very dramatic. I'd love to read the book. Is it published? If it's not in English, I'll get someone to translate it for me.'

Handa shook his head. 'I didn't write it for money. The manuscript is still in my house.'

'What a pity,' she said.

'He doesn't mind, do you, Handa?'

This came from Suri. He had, I gathered, a master's degree in English from the Punjab University. Later he took over his family's textile factory in Jullundur. He was on his way to clinch a business deal with his major wholesale customer in the South. He had got Handa, the son of an old friend and neighbour of his, to accompany him.

'Are both your daughters married, Mummy?' asked Handa.

'Oh yes.'

'To Anglo-Indian boys?'

'Who else, man?' put in Suri. 'Anglo-Indians only marry Anglo-Indians. They are Christians, but they won't choose even an Indian Christian as a marriage partner. I know because I was in Agra for a year, where there is quite a concentration of Anglo-Indians.'

'Yes, what you say applies to most of us,' said Mummy. 'My younger girl, though, is married not to an Anglo-Indian but to a Parsi engineer in Bombay. Things are changing. In the past we identified with a

British "home" that we had only known from hearsay. And when Independence came in 1947, some of us went to settle in England, including myself. But I realized that the English did not accept me as one of them, so I came back. There is only India left to us now. And, like you, we are Indian nationals.'

'What about your sons, Mummy?' asked Handa. 'Have they all got wives?'

'Four of them are married. But the fifth, who is in Australia, is single.'

'Do you know what questions have to be settled before a Hindu or Sikh engagement ceremony can take place?' he said. 'In Madras the parents of the boy ask if the girl wears her hair long and knows how to sing. In Bengal they ask if she wears her hair long and has a pond full of fish. But in the Punjab the girl's parents ask not about the boy's salary, but about the perks attached to his job.'

'So it comes down, in the end, to one thing: money,' remarked Mummy.

'No money, no honey,' said Suri. 'You Anglo-Indians are lucky people. Your boys and girls just go to a church and get married: it's a simple private affair attended by the families of the couple and some close friends. With us Hindus and Sikhs, however, a wedding is a ruinously expensive and complicated social occasion. You have to request the presence of all your near and distant relatives, as well as that of everybody in your neighbourhood and at your place of work. Miss out even a single one of them, and you have an enemy for life. The number of guests at a wedding can range from 100 to 500. We are crushed by the burden of old customs and traditions, and yet we dare not do away with them. Our society must change. The economy is in a mess: businesses going bankrupt, rising prices, higher taxes, unemployment – the list is endless.'

'It's inflation,' said Mummy. 'It's all over the world. Nobody knows how to bring it down.'

'There's that slogan: "Produce Less Children",' said Suri. 'But the people who spread it are called murderers of the future generations.'

'What is surprising about that?' Handa said. 'Such ideas are OK; the trouble is with the methods. In one case, for instance, the police rounded up twenty men from their houses late at night and drove them to a clinic, where they were forced to have an operation to sterilize them. Among this group was a man of 75, a great-grandfather. Now, isn't that a scandal? Birth control should be voluntary. There should be mass education.'

'And how long will it take to educate over six hundred million people?' Suri asked. 'Not less than half a century. Meanwhile the population will double or treble. No, I am for compulsory birth control. There should be a law to sterilize every man in the country after the birth of his second child. That is the first step in the right direction. Then we can tackle inflation and other economic problems.'

Handa laughed.

'Inflation,' he said, 'is like age. You can't stop getting older just as you can't bring the cost of living down. But if you do what one family did, then it's different.'

'What family are you talking about?' Suri asked.

'Be patient and you will know. One evening a man went home after work and found a young woman there. He wondered who she was, so he greeted her hesitantly, addressing her as "sister". She said: "I am your mother." He said: "I am 26 and you seem to be 25, so how can you be my mother?" She said: "But I am your mother." He said: "Well, if you are my mother, then where is my father?" She pointed to a child she was holding on her lap. "This," she said, "is your father." He said: "I don't know which of us is crazy. I don't understand anything." She said: "Well, you see, it was like this. I got up in the morning with a terrible headache. I looked for an aspirin in the cupboard where you keep such things, and took one. Then your father said he had a worse headache, so he swallowed two pills. There were only three of them in a yellow box." "The yellow box!" cried the young man, who was assistant to a chemist. "The pills in it: I got them from my boss as a reward for the way I do my job. Each pill, he told me, would make the user twenty-five years younger. You had one, so you became half your age. Father had two, and he became 5 years old." '

All this time the red-haired man next to Mummy had been occupied with his reading and note-taking. Sometimes he shook his head with an air of impatience, so that the yellow ring in his nostril danced about the left-hand corner of his mouth.

'Where do you think he is from?' Handa asked me in Punjabi, his mother tongue and also mine.

When a ticket examiner had been in our compartment earlier, the redhead had enquired in English about a train connection.

'From his accent he is probably Dutch or German,' I told Handa, who then asked:

'Can you guess what he is?'

A pair of dividers dangled from between the man's teeth; he was adding some details to a sketch of the planets' positions spread on his knees.

'Seems to be a scientist,' I replied.

'There are about fifteen hundred scientists who have come from abroad to watch tomorrow's eclipse,' said Handa. 'He must be one of them. Have you ever looked at an eclipse?'

'Oh, once – long ago. Through a piece of smoked glass. What I saw was just a patch of dull light, though people said it was a wonder of nature.'

'But the eclipse tomorrow is a rare phenomenon,' Suri commented. 'There was one like it eighty-two years ago, and the next eclipse isn't expected before the end of the century. That is why this one is of such world-wide interest. It will be possible to observe a total eclipse along a 130-kilometre-wide belt which extends for 1500 kilometres across the Deccan peninsula. Indian and foreign astronomers are gathering there to carry out experiments during the 135 minutes of the eclipse – from 2.36 p.m. to 4.51 p.m. It's all in the papers.'

There was, indeed, something odd about some of the forthcoming experiments. Scientists from the Bee Research Institute at Poona, for instance, were accompanying a colony of half a million bees to Gorkana in Andhra Pradesh to observe the behaviour of scout bees during the eclipse. Ornithologists were to study in the Bastiar jungle the way the exotic lorikeet bird holds itself topsy-turvy when the moon obscures the sun. And a team of American scientists was arriving in Ankola to see how monkeys react to eclipses.

'I think the media are making too much of this eclipse business,' remarked Mummy.

'But it is the sensation of the century after all,' argued Suri. 'The event is full of portents – not only for Hindus and Sikhs, but for the Muslims also and perhaps for other communities as well. You know what can happen if Rahu does not spit out the sun tomorrow? This world will be left in darkness.'

'Who is Rahu?'

'Our Handa here is an expert on legends. Come on, Handa!'

'One day Lord Vishnu was distributing *amrit* among the gods,' Handa began.

'*Amrit*,' Suri explained for Mummy's benefit, 'is the nectar of immortality. Carry on, Handa.'

'Well,' Handa resumed, 'there was a demon hiding near them. He had four arms and a tail. He slipped in between the gods and received some *amrit* in his cup. The fraud, however, was promptly detected by the Sun and Moon, who were in that group. They reported the matter to Vishnu. So Vishnu threw his discus and cut him in two. But the demon had already drunk the *amrit*: he was now immortal. His head became Rahu and his trunk became Ketu; both parts took their place among the stars and planets. Rahu has a chariot with eight black horses. In it, with his mouth wide open, he hunts through the sky for his old enemies, the Sun and Moon. Whenever he catches and swallows either of them, there is an eclipse.'

'Hm,' Mummy politely said.

'Didn't Handa tell the story rather well?' asked Suri.

'Oh, it's most interesting,' she said with emphasis. 'But don't you think the press is over-dramatizing the occasion?'

'Drama, Mummy, is the life-blood of journalism.'

'I know, but such a lot of incredible stuff is being written about the harm the eclipse might do.'

'The border-line between the credible and the incredible tends to be arbitrary,' remarked Suri with a teasing smile.

'Yes, but it's crazy, what the papers are doing.'

'How do you mean?'

'They seem to have put the country in a state of fever,' she declared. 'Astrologers and quacks are back in business, playing on the popular superstitions. Suddenly green bangles are everywhere in demand, costing four times their usual price, because they are believed to act as a protection against the evil influence of the eclipse. And people are being told to stay indoors, especially pregnant women who, we are warned, are particularly exposed to danger. Then again, public meetings are to be held round sacrificial fires in most cities during the eclipse. The central government hasn't helped things either by declaring tomorrow a public holiday. Really, it's just like pushing the panic button.'

Suri drew a newspaper out of his brief-case.

'All the same, there are scientific reasons why we should be careful tomorrow,' he said seriously. 'This, for example, is what the *Times of India* says on its front page: "Please resist the temptation or curiosity to look at the sun during the eclipse. Even the most fleeting glance can damage your eyes permanently".'

Turning to another page of the same paper, he went on:

'Ah, here it is! This is an advertisement, on behalf of the central government, from the Ministry of Science and Technology. A solar eclipse, it says causes "an exciting feeling which will have to be experienced rather than described".' He skipped some words. 'And it concludes: "Throughout the period of the eclipse, please take yourself away from the sun to avoid the possibility of looking into the sun." To treat the people who foolishly ignore these warnings and ruin their eyes, special eye clinics have been set up all over the country.'

I fell asleep. A sudden thump woke me up. It was the tough-looking chap with the twirled moustache, who had jumped off the bunk he had been lying on. The train gave a lurch and started moving. I was just in time to see him snatch up his mini-suitcase and dash out of the carriage.

'Where is Mummy?' I asked as the train picked up speed.

'She got off at the last station,' Suri answered from the bunk below mine. 'That character who was up there watching her is after her. He must have dozed off, so he didn't see her leaving. But he'll catch up with her, I'm sure.'

'Poor Mummy,' said Handa from the bottom bunk. 'I did warn her against him. She was wearing bangles of solid gold.'

'He won't be able to get her bangles off in a hurry,' Suri said. 'I think he will first have a go at the gold necklace she had on.'

'Or her handbag,' said Handa. 'It was made of snakeskin. Looked imported.'

'Her son in Australia must have sent it to her,' said Suri. 'Imported articles, even if they are of the worst quality, fetch high prices.'

'She told me she was going to visit her sister,' said Handa. 'I asked if she had sent her a telegram about her arrival. She said she had not, but hoped she'd get a taxi. I don't think she will find one easily: it was a small station, deserted-looking and rather badly lit. And that thief of a fellow seemed to be a nasty type.'

'Well, we can't help her now,' said Suri. 'Let's try and get some sleep.'

Morning came. There was a touch of coolness in the air. The European with the nose ring had gone. New passengers had got on. Beyond the window, sunshine alternated with cloud. We were flying past groves of mangoes, date palms, tamarinds and coconut trees. A bamboo copse gave way to a banana plantation on the edge of a village where people were already at work in the fields. Mist-topped hills in the distance kept appearing and disappearing. They belonged, as Suri said in reply to Handa's question, to the mountain range of the Eastern Ghats.

A Southern Railway attendant entered the compartment. The red

badge on the breast of his white jacket showed his name below the words TRAIN SERVER. He approached a middle-aged couple, who turned out to be from Kerala.

'You want to order lunch?' he asked in English.

The husband bared his yellow uneven teeth, lifting his pale eyes. 'What lunch is it?' he enquired.

'Non-vegetarian.'

'Not vegetarian?'

'No,' answered the train server briskly. 'Non-vegetarian only.'

The husband looked disappointed and seemed to grow angry.

'Then we don't want anything,' he said, waving the other away.

Suri, who was a member of the meat-eating Sikh community, gave an ironical smile and a slight shake of his head.

It was not yet noon when the train drew into Tiruchirapalli (formerly Trichinopoly), a major railway junction. Madras was still some 400 kilometres away. I wiped the film of sweat that had formed on my upper lip again. My discomfort, which must have been evident, amused Suri.

'Wait till you get to Madras,' he said.

'What's the weather like there?' I asked.

'It's said to be three months hot and nine months hotter.'

'But the sea breezes, don't they lessen the heat?'

'All they give you is an illusion of coolness.'

A handcart stopped outside our window. On it stood two barrel-shaped containers. They had lengths of hemp rope wound round them tightly to keep the contents from getting warm. A young woman in a white sari filled a glass from a tap fitted to one of the containers. She handed it over the window-sill to me.

'How's the water?' asked Suri.

'Nice and cool,' I answered, returning the empty glass to the woman. She shook her head in refusal when I held out a coin to her.

'It's free of charge,' Suri told me, indicating to the woman that he wanted a drink as well.

From a passing railway official I learned that the train would remain in Tiruchirapalli for another half an hour. Leaving the carriage, I strolled leisurely down the long platform. A woman was selling white and yellow jasmine from a large round basket. As I caught a whiff of their fragrance, I reflected that it was probably the first time I had seen cut flowers on sale on a station platform in India.

I suddenly stopped near a bookstall. In front of it a beefy man of 30 or 35 was knocking about a much younger chap half his size. Behind him were four or five of his admiring supporters. A smile lit up his eyes and a grin showed his white teeth a couple of times when he pretended to land a blow on his victim's nose, so that the other flinched as he shielded his tear-stained face with his arm, uttering a scared, croaky yell. He would then tap the small fellow's unguarded head with the wooden handle of a short metal bar he carried in one hand.

Two uniformed men with truncheons stood by, looking rather amused; they wore badges with the letters TRP – Tamil Nadu Railway Police. I was struck by the grins and encouraging noises that kept coming from the old man behind the bookstall counter.

The small chap wore an open shirt over tight-fitting trousers that had lost their crease. All his pockets were turned inside out. He was still whimpering when a fierce-looking man with a clipped moustache strode up. He exchanged a glance with the beefy man, apparently his superior, who nodded to him. He shouted at the small chap, struck out wildly, then dragged him away, punching and slapping him all the while. A little crowd formed behind them. Occasional screams floated back from a distance. The policemen drifted off. One of them hollered something in reply to a railway official who had probably asked what the row had been about. The explanation was greeted with a nod and a laugh by the other.

Displayed on the bookstall was a book: *Our Heritage* by Radhakrishnan, the philosopher and former president of India (1962–67). And I remembered reading in the *Handbook of India* – a tourist guide brought out by the Publications Division of the Ministry of Information and Broadcasting – about Tiruchirapalli being famous for its seventh-century cave temples and varied cultural achievements.

As I turned round, I ran into my two travelling companions who had watched the whole scene.

'Did you see the policemen?' Handa asked me. 'They didn't intervene even once. Instead, they just looked on, smiling from time to time as if to egg that big fat bully on.'

'I only know a few words of Tamil,' remarked Suri. 'The little fellow, it seemed, was suspected of theft. But even if he was guilty, that was no way to go about the matter. People in the South are considered to be mild. But this shows how brutal they can sometimes be.'

'I felt bad about not helping the boy,' I confessed.

'Thank God you didn't step in,' said Handa. 'We are just passing through. It's no good getting mixed up in other people's quarrels. After all, we're strangers here.'

We set off again. Not long afterwards Handa and Suri parted company with me. The dry, hot afternoon wore on. Madras was now only about ninety minutes away. The landscape outside the window continued to change. We skirted a lake, then rushed along through a forest of coconut and palmyra palms. A view of the sea was succeeded by a glimpse of the red-roofed houses of a settlement with mangrove and fir trees stretching into the distance. The train kept stopping at the smallest of stations. Most of the new passengers seemed to be local people or commuters. The tickets were being inspected with greater frequency.

The man checking them was in the regulation uniform – a two-piece suit of blue serge. The somewhat loose fit of his clothes, together with the contented look on his black plump face, suggested that he was relaxed and good-natured. I thought of having a little chat with him.

As he was a travelling ticket examiner, he had a compartment all to himself. He was perched on a long seat. Next to him lay a peaked cap and a clipboard with papers on it. He withdrew the tip of his tongue with which he was moistening the crust on his lower lip. The brown, almond-shaped eyes flashed me a greeting. Then came the usual question about where I came from and what I did for a living. As to himself, he was a native of Madras. I asked whether Tamil, which was his language, and Malayalam, which is spoken in Kerala, were closely related.

He shook his head of close-cropped greying hair.

'Even their scripts are entirely different,' he declared.

'But you understand Malayalam, don't you?'

'Not at all.'

'It's hard to believe that, since your people and those of Kerala are practically neighbours. Wasn't Malayalam originally a dialect of Tamil?'

'Maybe a thousand years ago. They have nothing in common with each other now, except that they both belong to South India.'

I told him about the trouble I had had in getting a booking to Delhi.

'You made a mistake,' was his comment. 'You should have gone to the train supervisor of the KK Express in Trivandrum and given him some money. He would have fixed you up with a seat at once.'

'I didn't know that,' I said. 'What do you advise me to do on reaching Madras?'

'Bribe the reservation people,' was his prompt reply. 'I bribe them myself when I want to reserve a seat. The train gets into Egmore – that is the terminal station – at about 7 p.m. Go straight from there to the booking-office at the Central Station. It is open till 8 p.m. only.'

'But how much should I pay – the bribe, I mean?'

The travelling ticket examiner looked at me in some surprise, as if he thought me naïve. Then he smiled with an air of tolerance and said:

'They will let you know themselves – they are clever people.'

I returned to my compartment. Seated opposite me was a Kerala man with a woman who might have been his wife or mother. I thanked him for having kept an eye on my luggage during my brief absence. He had told me that he worked in Madras. I now asked him if he could suggest where I should stay in that city.

'There are many hotels near the Central Station,' he replied. 'But I would recommend the Vikram Hotel. It's run by Mr Poti, a Brahman gentleman from Kerala. You always get value for money there. It's in Wall Tax Street, a five-minute walk from the station.'

When I got off the train at Egmore Station, it was already 7.30. The station approach was thick with people and vehicles of all descriptions. I jumped into the first taxi that came my way. The promise of a tip as big as the fare put the driver in such an adventurous mood that he whirled me off to the Central Station in less than ten minutes. The second-class booking-office was on an upper floor. There were only three or four people before me. A European girl wanted to buy two tickets, but the clerk was declining to accept a traveller's cheque she was holding out to him.

'You must cash it at a bank,' he told her.

'But the banks are closed now,' she argued. 'And tomorrow is a public holiday. So they're closed tomorrow as well.'

'Yes, because of the eclipse, I know,' he admitted. 'But I can't take payment in foreign currency or traveller's cheques.'

I used this opportunity to present my ticket to him as I made my request. He slipped me a reservation application form. I filled it out quickly and handed it back. He took a look at it and nodded.

'But you must have a confirmation on your ticket – that you've broken your journey,' he then said.

'Where do I get that?'

'The excess fare counter downstairs – in the main hall.' And squinting at the wall clock above him: 'We are closing exactly in six minutes.'

I raced down the steps. The many offices in the large, illuminated hall confused me for a moment. Suddenly, however, I was standing before the counter I wanted. The young woman behind it had bright-red lips; the smile of amusement that twitched at their corners had no doubt been provoked by the note of panic in my voice and tense look on my face. In half a minute, though, she had scribbled a couple of words on the back of my ticket – important words that were nonetheless as hard to make out as those on a doctor's prescription.

I was out of breath when I got back to the booking-office upstairs. There was a man in front of it.

'We are closed now,' I heard the clerk tell him. 'Come tomorrow.'

'But are you open tomorrow?' asked the other.

'Of course we are open. And the trains are running on time too.'

'Even during the eclipse?'

'Yes, even during the eclipse. Our drivers don't look at the sun when they are on duty. They look at the tracks, you know.'

I pressed my face to the grille.

'Do you remember me?' I said to the clerk. 'I was here a moment ago. You asked me to get a confirmation. The excess fare counter has given it.'

He snatched the ticket from my fingers and, barely glancing at the endorsement, dropped it on his desk. Then he got busy with some paperwork. I was reminded of the advice given by the travelling ticket examiner on the train earlier that evening: 'Bribe the reservation people. I bribe them myself . . .'

So I took the plunge.

'I'll be glad to make you a little cash present for the favour you're doing me.'

The clerk, a slim long-haired man in his mid-thirties, knit his brows, putting down his pen. The bristles covering his face hinted that he had not shaved that day. He turned to me with an ironical look.

'Here is your ticket and reservation,' he said in a crisp voice. 'It is only on certain days that I accept cash presents,' he added, shutting the window. 'Today isn't one of them.'

Leaving the station, I turned left and found myself in Wall Tax Street. At once I set out to find the Vikram Hotel which the Kerala man on the train had spoken highly of. But the noise and congestion around did not suit my present mood. I felt very tired. A couple of passers-by I asked mentioned some hotels in the immediate neighbourhood, so I turned down a narrow side-street. The first place I enquired at had no room free; the second suggested trying a hotel further along the street.

As I went out of its entrance, a small but muscular man came up to me. He wore a red uniform with the badge of a railway porter. He offered to carry my suitcase. I shook my head and walked on, with him close at my heels. Stopping under a street-light, I told him I did not need his services. He said something in Tamil, then grabbed at my suitcase, but I swung it out of his reach.

A look of injured dignity came over his square, tight-skinned face. His handlebar moustache, blue-black in the fluorescent light, quivered as he suddenly began gesticulating. A rush of words came from him. Only two of them, which were in English, did I take in: 'No money.' They implied that he was ready to carry the case for nothing. I refused.

I was making my way down the street through an area of partial darkness when he reappeared at my side. He tried to relieve me of the suitcase. I shook him off. He tried again, but missed. Hoping to make him behave himself, I warned him:

'I'll report you to the police.'

This somehow sank in. His reaction was immediate.

'Police!' he spat out, jeering at me. 'Police!'

Moving back a couple of steps, he raised his fists and challenged me to a fight. When I did not respond, he went through the motions of a boxer punching his opponent.

There was a bend in the street some fifty paces away. Lights were burning there. I decided to head for them. But he was blocking my way and seemed likely to turn violent. He did not, however, touch me as I went past him. I walked fast. But he overtook me as I reached the bend. Pausing, he bowed to me, then ran forward and entered a hotel. I followed him in. It turned out that he had already spoken on my behalf. Before I could get a word out, the manager told me:

'I know what you want, sir, but we are fully booked up right now.'

Back in the street, I had to endure the man's company again. He virtually danced around me. Now he was behind me, now in front, trying to find me accommodation at each of the hotels we came to. Evidently he was hoping to make a little money on the side: if he got me a room, he could claim a fee not only from the hotel management, but perhaps from me also. Then, to my surprise, he vanished as suddenly as he had appeared.

By this time, however, I had miraculously re-emerged into Wall Tax Street. The noise and congestion around were no better than before, but they no longer bothered me; on the contrary, I was grateful for them. The sight of a neon sign at the side of a building brought me up short. What, was it possible that the place I had set out to find was now staring me right in the face? The sign flashed on again: THE VIKRAM HOTEL.

My hopes rose.

The hotel front stood flush with the street. I went up the two narrow cement steps before the door, crossed the threshold and was immediately in the oblong entrance hall. At the reception desk sat a tall, handsome man in his early forties. The material and cut of his suit suggested good taste and money. The sacred mark on his forehead was made up of a thumb-sized dab of red paste. My fellow passenger on the train had remarked that the hotel was run by a Kerala Brahman, so the man before me was probably the manager or the owner of the establishment.

'Good evening, Mr Poti!'

As he returned my greeting, he seemed slightly puzzled by the cheerful and almost intimate tone of voice in which I had addressed him.

'Do we know each other?' he asked.

'At least I know you – indirectly, though,' I replied. 'I've just arrived from Kottayam, in Kerala.'

'Kottayam? I am a native of that city.'

'Someone I met there told me to come to you whenever I needed accommodation in Madras,' I said, encouraged by the turn the conversation was taking. 'He rather looked like you – as if he were a relative of yours.'

'What was his name?'

'Oh, his name was . . . Sorry, it has escaped my memory.'

'It must have been one of my two cousins who live in Kottayam. Well, in that case, let me see what I can do for you.'

His eyes narrowed in thought. An involuntary movement of his hand indicated the flights of stairs to his right.

'Yes, on the fifth floor,' he went on. 'It's not the best of our rooms, but it's the only one I can give you at the moment. I'll ask a servant to get it ready for you to move in.'

He pressed a bell, then gestured towards a couple of chairs along the wall at the far end.

'Please make yourself at home meanwhile.'

I took my seat. I was facing a door that opened on to an inner court where, as I observed later, Mr Poti and his family occupied a couple of suites. A shortish man came through it into the reception hall, in response to his employer's summons. He received his orders in Malayalam. There was no lift; he climbed the stairs to tidy up the room intended for me.

'This street of yours,' I said to Mr Poti, 'has an odd sort of name. Why is it called Wall Tax Street?'

'Historical associations,' he replied in his even, pleasant-sounding voice. 'In the late eighteenth or early nineteenth century the East India Company, which governed Madras, started building a city wall here. A tax was imposed on every household within the wall to meet the cost of its construction. It caused a storm of protests. The matter was referred to Bengal, which was then under the direct rule of the British Government. And Bengal eventually decided against the tax the Company had levied on the inhabitants. There are some remains of the old wall close by. You may see them tomorrow if you like.'

'I want to make the most of tomorrow, as I intend to leave the day after. Could you give me an idea of the places worth visiting?'

'Tomorrow isn't an auspicious day for sightseeing,' Mr Poti remarked a trifle solemnly.

My glance drifted to the gods and goddesses framed on the wall behind him. The largest picture there was of a round-faced man with gentle eyes and a long white beard. It was festooned with flowers. A number of Indians, particularly Hindus, put themselves in the charge of someone they consider wise and holy, who answers their spiritual and psychological needs. They accept his guidance in much the same way as people in the West accept the guidance of their psychoanalysts.

'Your guru?' I asked, pointing to the picture.

A look of devotion came over Mr Poti's face as he regarded the person in the frame.

'Yes, my guru,' he said. 'A true saint. My family and I obey him implicitly.'

'You said it was inauspicious to go sightseeing tomorrow. Because of the eclipse?'

'Exactly. Besides, you won't be able to see much. It's an official holiday tomorrow, you know. All public transport will stop by midday. No afternoon postal delivery either. Even the zoo will close at noon. And you won't be able to enter or leave the hotel from 1.30 to 6 p.m.'

'Oh, is that so?'

'Yes, the main door will stay closed during that period.'

'You mean you're going to lock yourself in?'

'Of course! I'm a religious man. We'll neither eat nor cook any food for the duration. And we'll burn incense sticks in each of the hotel rooms to ward off the evil influence of the eclipse.'

The man who had gone upstairs to clean up my room was back.

'So I'll have to make an early start if everything is coming to a halt by noon,' I remarked. 'Will you get someone to wake me up at five in the morning?'

'No problem,' Mr Poti said, making a note of my request on a piece of paper. He handed me a key he had taken off a hook projecting from a rack, then stuck the note on the empty hook.

The air in my low-ceilinged, L-shaped room was stuffy. I switched on the fan. The window gave on to a backyard. I flung it open, only to shut it, for fear of letting mosquitoes in. By the sickly light of the overhead bulb, I made out a narrow bed, a steel chair and a broken-down old harmonium on a three-legged table in a corner. I had not had a proper wash since the previous day. An alcove at the other end of the room served as a bathroom of a sort. Throwing off my clothes, I stepped across its cement floor on to a low wooden bench. I turned the tap on. The bucket under it filled up quickly. Using the mug lying next to it, I started pouring water on me. The feeling of heat and tiredness drained away at last. Tiny, seed-like objects clung to the bedspread in places. I peeled it off and dropped it to the floor. The sheet, which had some yellow stains, met with the same fate. Covering myself with my old dressing gown, I fell asleep almost at once.

Suddenly the sun was shining at the window. I bathed hurriedly.

There was no time for my morning yoga. Downstairs Mr Poti looked fresh and spruce at the reception desk.

'I asked to be woken at five o'clock,' I said. 'But nobody knocked on my door.'

'Oh?' He assumed an air of surprise. 'But I did leave instructions to that effect. Sorry.'

Asked, he mentioned some places of interest I might visit. Then he sent one of his staff to find transport for me.

Only now did I become aware of a man in a soutane who had come down the stairs and was standing near me.

'Pardon me, but I happened to overhear part of your conversation,' he said to me. 'I would like to make a suggestion if you don't mind.'

He was a person of great height, with severe, almost forbidding features. I was, however, impressed by the note of sweetness in his voice.

'Please go ahead.'

'I am a Catholic priest, but, like you, a visitor here. I was at the Cathedral of St Thomas yesterday, and that moved me deeply. You must see it without fail.'

'What is special about it?'

'St Thomas, who brought Christianity to India, is buried there.'

'Did he die in Madras?'

'Yes, he was martyred here on St Thomas's Mount in AD 68. The local people resented his preaching. A Brahman is said to have killed him with a lance while he was praying. You can see the relics of the lance in the cathedral, which is in Mylapore, about 11 kilometres from Egmore Station. Madras, you see, has close links with Christianity, even though its population is predominantly Hindu. The cathedral was founded by the Portuguese in the sixteenth century. It is a magnificent building – historically of extraordinary value, and for us Christians a holy shrine. You may go there after your sightseeing trip – even in the afternoon, when Madras will probably look like a ghost town.'

'You mean it's open during the eclipse?'

'Of course! In the past, you know, the Christians too believed in evil omens concerned with eclipses. Even the ancient Greeks and Romans believed in them. There was, for instance, an Athenian general by the name of Nicias. Though he was a brave man and dynamic leader, he refused to fight the Syracusans because of an eclipse of the moon that night. So what happened? The enemy slaughtered his entire army and killed him as well. That was in 413 BC. Long, long ago. The modern Christians –'

'Your rickshaw is here,' Mr Poti broke in.

'Excuse me,' I said to the priest, who gave an understanding nod and went out. I had a glimpse of him as he paused in the street and, by way of a blessing, stroked the hood of a rickshaw that had just drawn up in front of the hotel.

The driver came in. He was a well set-up chap of about 20, in a khaki shirt worn over khaki shorts.

'But I asked for an autorickshaw,' I told Mr Poti. 'I wanted to travel at speed and take in as many places as possible.'

He explained my objection to the driver, then translated the other's reaction to me:

'The man says that an autorickshaw is like an aeroplane that shows you nothing of your surroundings as it flies. But if you are in a bicycle rickshaw you will get a good view of the things as you go.'

'He's probably right,' I said. 'But I have so little time at my disposal.'

'My servant couldn't find anything else. Better take this rickshaw. I'll give the driver a list of the places he should take you to. He seems to be an honest type of fellow.'

'Well, in that case, let us hire him.'

The driver mentioned his price for the trip.

'Don't you think it's a bit too steep?' I asked Mr Poti.

'Quite so,' he agreed. 'But it's a special day, you know. I doubt if you will be able to get hold of anyone who will charge less.'

'OK then.'

'And he says you'll have to buy him breakfast or lunch.'

'What?' I said. 'Oh, well, in for a penny, in for a pound. Does he speak any Hindi or English?'

'No, Tamil only. But he knows what he has to do. And he dare not cheat you. I have already taken precautions. I have told him that he will get his money when he brings you back to the hotel. His name, by the way, is Manohar.'

Folding the list he had received from Mr Poti, Manohar the rickshaw driver slipped it into the pocket of his open shirt. We moved off. The muscles of his calves bulged as his bare feet pressed the pedals. He seemed to be in a light-hearted mood and was humming a tune. The clock tower of the Central Station showed 7.30. Soon we were in the main commercial section of the city. The rickshaw wove in and out of the traffic along Mount Road. Suddenly Manohar jumped off his saddle. He looked worried as he examined the front wheel.

'Why, what's happened?' I asked.

He pointed to the tyre. It had punctured. He led the rickshaw over to a repair shop. It was some time before the puncture was mended – at my expense of course! We set off again, only to stop a quarter of an hour later. Perched on the saddle, Manohar turned round to face me. He was saying something and at the same time making gestures. I gathered that he wanted to have a bite. I was not hungry yet. It occurred to me, however, that no eating-place might be open from noon onwards. So I gave in.

The restaurant where we pulled up was large and well appointed. Manohar strode down its tiled floor with a look of assurance. We entered one of the booths along the wall to the right. The menu was in both English and Tamil. The dish he chose cost twice as much as the one I ordered. Breakfast over, I felt like a smoke. He pointed a forefinger at the packet I had opened. I offered it to him. Calmly he withdrew two cigarettes. He slid one into his shirt pocket. The other he lit and puffed at it with an air of satisfaction.

After about an hour I remembered the phone call old Bhullar, the under-secretary, had made the evening before I left Delhi: 'Don't miss the Snake Park in Madras'. And now I was at the entrance to the very place. Manohar let me understand that he wanted to come along too, so I bought two entrance tickets.

We approached one of the outdoor terrariums. It was open at the top, with a parapet running round. Manohar leaned over and gazed down its steep, concrete sides. He drew back with a start. The scene at the bottom, which was alive with a multitude of snakes, had obviously scared him. His glance met mine. For a moment he looked as if he were ashamed of the fear he had betrayed. Then he smiled – simply, trustingly. I was beginning to like him.

In a nearby enclosure, with the forked trunk of a tree planted down its middle, an attendant sat on a steel chair. The dark stubble on his chin was flecked with grey, and his eyes were half-closed. Manohar seemed to regard him with surprise, because next to the steel chair a full-grown python lay coiled and motionless on the earthen floor.

'Isn't it dangerous staying so close to such a big snake?' I asked the attendant.

'This one is as harmless as a baby,' he answered serenely.

There were two more visitors there: a trim handsome young man in the company of a slim girl with delicate features and large, radiant eyes.

'Just because it has been tamed,' remarked the young man. 'An untamed python, though non-poisonous, can be highly dangerous. It twists itself round its prey and crushes it to death. But pythons are easy to tame, you know.'

'Really?' I said.

'Yes,' the girl spoke in a lilting voice, 'they are quite easy to tame.'

'And they are full of vitamins,' he declared.

'That's cold comfort to their victims,' I said.

'No, I mean they are good to eat,' he explained.

'Sounds a bit far-fetched.'

'But it's a fact. Python meat is considered to be a delicacy in many countries – in China, for instance, in Japan, Vietnam, Hong Kong and elsewhere. It's of a pale colour and tastes just like chicken.'

'That's right,' came from his companion softly.

'And it's supposed to do wonders for one's virility,' he said.

'Have you tried it?' I asked.

'No, but I know people who have,' he replied.

We went on together. His bearing was upright and he moved with elastic grace. In reply to my question, he told me that he was from Nagpur, a city in Maharashtra state, and a lieutenant in the army. He had already looked over the snake park.

'There are fine specimens of reptiles here,' he said. 'You have cobras, kraits, puff adders and pythons, as well as flying snakes – these flatten themselves against the branches of a tree and slide through the little opening among the leaves. Also, salt-water snakes and freshwater snakes. And then you have giant tortoises, monitor lizards . . .'

'You know such a lot,' I said. 'Did you study zoology?'

'No, but I was a commando in the jungles of Assam,' he explained. 'I'm trained to catch and kill snakes.'

The girl beamed at him:

'And you can kill even cobras.'

'Of course I can.'

'How does one do that?' I asked him.

He stopped on the gravel path we had taken.

'You need two sticks,' he explained. 'A short one with a forked end to

102

grip and hold the cobra's head down, and a long one to twist its body round, so as to have its tail pressed firmly under one foot.'

'But that calls for courage,' I put in.

'Once you have mastered the skill, it becomes a routine operation,' he said.

'Could you kill a cobra?' I asked the girl.

'Not me,' she answered shyly though not without pride, 'but he can.'

'I'll show you how it's done,' he said.

Standing with his legs wide apart, he bent forward and set out to illustrate his two-stick method. There was an expression of childlike wonder in Manohar's eyes as they followed each movement the other made. The lieutenant created the illusion of imprisoning the neck as well as the tail of a cobra before crushing its head with his free foot.

'Have you killed many?' I asked.

'Well, actually there weren't a lot of cobras around when I was with the commando unit in Assam,' he confessed. 'And actually it was my fellow officers who for the most part were lucky enough to catch those that could be seen. But I watched how they finished them off with two sticks.'

'He knows the technique,' said the girl. 'And that, after all, is what really matters.'

'Are you two engaged?' I asked.

'We were once,' she answered cheerfully. 'We are on our honeymoon just now.'

The rickshaw still stood where we had left it near the entrance. Manohar started back along a metalled track. Just as we were turning into the main road, he stopped. He walked across the sunlit verge to a woman under an acacia tree. She sat on a mat, with her back held erect. The old wrinkled face bore the same patient look I had noticed on my way to the snake park. Bits of sugar candy and coconut kernel were laid out on a wooden tray before her. The spot being deserted, the chances of her finding a customer for her goods seemed to be very slim indeed.

I was still thinking about the woman's silent courage in the face of a hopeless situation when I saw Manohar give her a coin. She chose some pieces of sugar candy and coconut meat for him; but he made a gesture even as he said something to her, so that she put them back on the tray. He returned to the rickshaw, looking very cheerful, as if pleased with his good deed. I envied him at that moment.

'Were you at the lighthouse?' Mr Poti asked me at the hotel.

'Yes, I was.'

'Did you notice how high it is? Forty-nine metres exactly. You can see its light well over 30 kilometres off at sea.'

'I didn't go up. It was closed.'

'And the aquarium?'

'The same. Closed.'

'It's a pity,' he said. 'But I did warn you that you would not have much luck today.'

His glance went to the clock on the wall: it read ten to one.

'We are locking the main door in forty minutes,' he added. 'It will be unlocked at six.'

'That means four and a half hours. How do you intend to spend the time?'

'In prayer and meditation.'

'All the while?'

'Yes, of course. Rahu, the demon, is going to swallow the sun, and it is only our prayers that will get him to release it. But the guests who stay indoors needn't follow my example and that of my family. They can watch television if they like – a film is being specially shown in the afternoon.'

I went up to my room and washed quickly. What next? The prospect of being cooped up in the hotel for the rest of the day was far from tempting. So I shoved a small towel and some reading matter into a cloth bag, hung it on my shoulder and hurried out. Shortly afterwards I was crossing the broad forecourt of the Central Station.

The usual crowds of people were in the entrance hall. The large booking-hall, with its black-and-white tiled floor, was equally full. Fans hung from the high ceiling; their giant blades turned languidly. The snack-bars were all closed. Making my way past a row of offices, I went through an unguarded ticket barrier beyond which I could see the platforms. The roofed-in part of the station was brightly illuminated.

Going up a short flight of steps on my left, I came to a longish balcony. I noticed several retiring rooms at its end. Then I was standing before a restaurant. It was open. After some minutes, however, an announcement said it was unlikely that lunch would be served because of the impending eclipse. But just as I got up, having lost all hope, a waiter rushed over and brought me what I had ordered.

Downstairs, I wandered into the second-class waiting-room. It was full of people. Trunks, bedrolls and other articles of luggage lay all over the place. Some children were scampering about, laughing and shouting. A baby had left a little pool of urine on the floor. Two men were beating a drum. And a loudspeaker, fixed to one of the walls, was booming out the news, interspersed with railway announcements. The big lunch I had eaten and the racket around me made me feel tired. I found some empty space on one of the wooden benches. Using

my shoulder bag as a pillow, I lay down, picking up a brochure someone had left behind. I turned to its first page and read:

'The Indian railway system with its 60, 234 route-kilometres is the
largest in Asia. It is the second largest single system in the world.'

Sleepily I wondered which country had the largest single system in
the world.

'It is divided into nine zones,' the brochure continued. 'The Southern
zone, with its headquarters at Madras, has 7605 route-kilometres . . .
The rates for second-class passengers are the lowest in Asia.'

They were perhaps the lowest in the world, I thought. For a journey
of some 6000 kilometres I had paid the equivalent of £27. I dozed off.

The blast of an announcement from the loudspeaker startled me out
of my brief shut-eye. The children in the waiting-room were yelling
louder than ever and the drumbeat had risen to a crescendo. I sat up. A
boy of 15 or 16 had taken his place beside me. Pointing to my shoulder
bag, he said:

'Can I have it?'

'Why?' I asked, surprised.

'I want to put it under my head. Want to sleep a little.'

'But there are books in it.'

'You had it under your head too,' he said. 'Just for a little while,
please!'

I hesitated; but the way he had argued was logical, so I gave him the
bag. Hardly had his head touched it than he started snoring. I went out
into the main hall. The eclipse had begun an hour earlier, at 2.36 p.m.
The station forecourt and the streets were deserted and lay in dimmed
twilight. I dared myself to look up at the sun, but my courage failed me.
A man next to me was saying that he had seen a large flight of birds
moving across the sky only a few minutes before.

'They were going back to their nests for the night, I'm sure,' he
added.

I returned to the waiting-room. The boy was fast asleep. I eased my
bag away from under his head, putting a folded newspaper in its place.
He went on snoring peacefully. As I stepped out of the door, a little
group approached me. It was led by a tall young man. He looked
solemn. The young woman by his side had bobbed hair, her low-necked
dress showed off her figure to advantage. They walked arm in arm. A
matronly lady followed them. She was flanked by two pretty girls
whose unbound hair fell in glossy waves over their shoulders, down to
their waists.

The young man wore a dark tunic-like coat with a dark cap something like a truncated cone in shape. My guess – that he and his
companions were Parsis – turned out to be right. They are the

descendants of the Persians who fled to India in the eighth century AD
to escape Muslim persecution. They follow the teachings of Zoroaster,
who lived about the eighth century BC. Their faith prescribes physical
and moral purity. Fire, earth and water are the elements they honour.
As a result they do not either bury or cremate their dead. The corpse,
which is held to be impure, must not come into contact with any of
these elements; hence it is left to be devoured by vultures. There are
only about 150,000 Parsis in India, but their contribution to the
country's industrial, scientific, political and artistic progress has been
outstanding. They are well educated and their women enjoy social
freedom. They are generally very rich and known for their charitable
trusts and institutions. As a rule, however, they do not marry outside
their community. The devout ones among them, because of their
reverence for fire, are non-smokers.

The little group floated past me and I caught a whiff of perfume and
talcum powder. It seemed as if they were celebrating. They stopped at

a tea stall a couple of steps away. A beggar with a hideously swollen
eye went up and stretched out a hand towards them. The stallkeeper
warned him off. The young man alone, it appeared, had asked for tea.
He was just raising the cup to his lips when a brown dog emerged from
somewhere, snapped at him and ran away with a piece of his trouser
leg between its teeth. He broke out in shouts and curses.

'I am not to blame,' the stallkeeper was saying in his defence. 'It
must have happened because of the black suit you are wearing. The
ladies were not attacked, as their clothes are of another colour.'

'What rubbish!' retorted the young man. 'We are Parsis: we don't
believe in such things.'

'That is exactly the reason why you have made the gods angry. You
put on a black suit during the eclipse. So the dog came to punish you.'

Towards evening, an hour or so after the eclipse had ended, the
shops in the main street outside Central Station were open again. I

was trying to choose some picture postcards from a little stand placed outside a brightly lit bookstall. They were of so many kinds that I was hard put to it to make up my mind. I felt I was being watched. A man of about 40 stood in front of the neighbouring booth. He had just bought a betel leaf and lighted his cigarette with the smouldering end of a hemp rope suspended from a nail in the doorpost of the booth.

'Are you a Madras man?' I asked as he nodded me a greeting.

'Yes, I am.'

'I want to send some cards to friends in Europe. Can you recommend those that are typical of Madras?'

He asked to see the couple already in my hand. Then he shook his head.

'Pictures of modern buildings or of flyovers mean little to people in Europe,' he said. 'They have plenty of them. India to most of them is old temples, snake-charmers, yogis and the like. They simply can't imagine that we are also capable of technological achievements. And even if we were to make an atom bomb tomorrow, they would still think it had been done with Russian or American know-how. Better send your friends something that fits in with their image of India, and then they will be pleased.'

Asked, I told him about myself. There was a coffee bar next door. I accepted his invitation and we went in. He was in advertising, working for a company that did business with almost all the national newspapers. I mentioned the paper-borrowing habit I had noticed in Kerala.

'I like Kerala for its scenery and coconut palms,' he told me, 'but its roads are bad and its taxi drivers are cheats. Karnataka, another of our neighbouring states, is even worse in that respect. Of course some taxi drivers cheat here too, but they are severely punished if caught. One of them, for instance, charged a foreigner 130 rupees for a ride from the airport to the city; he was reported and jailed for three months.

'And as for borrowing newspapers, Kerala is notorious. People in Madras would never do that. I'll give you the example of a man staying at a hotel here. Every morning when he buys a paper, he splits it up into eight parts and divides them among his fellow hotel guests. They exchange these parts with one another until all of them have read the entire paper.'

'That's an original idea,' I said.

'One must care for people,' he said as if he had not heard my remark, 'especially when they come from another province or country. The other day I witnessed a curious thing. An autorickshaw driver wanted 10 rupees from a stranger for the journey between the Central Station and Egmore Station. I beat him down to the usual fare of 3 rupees.

Money is necessary, but it is not everything and one should not become its slave.'

'What did you do during the eclipse?' I asked.

'You know, I come from a priestly family and am a Brahman,' he replied, 'but it is only the scientific implications of the phenomenon that are important to me – infra-red or ultraviolet rays. Religious beliefs – like the one that an eclipse is produced by the demon Rahu swallowing the sun – are just stories. Science is progress. The old ideas go back to the times when people travelled in bullock carts only. If God is on the moon, how about the first man who got there? People say that God does everything, but there is a limit to that and we have to use our common sense.'

I was amazed next morning by the way the major Indian papers reported on the eclipse. 'Spectacle of the Century' declared one. 'Celestial Drama' announced another. 'The moon keeps its tryst with the sun and the stars twinkle in the afternoon', commented a third national daily in a poetical vein.

It was, however, the account in another newspaper that left me mystified: 'Thousands of people who were earlier tongue-tied without their knowing it, came back to their senses and started talking again.'

On my return to Delhi, I mentioned this to Fikr Taunsvi. He was so impressed by the piece of news that he exclaimed:

'That is all we need – still more people who can talk!'

*   *   *

My Indian encounters were ending for the time being; but there still remained something that was important to me – and then I found myself in a situation as strange as it was unexpected.

By the River of Salvation

It was late in the afternoon when the inter-city bus from Delhi brought me to Hardwar, in Uttar Pradesh state. This is the place where the holiest of Hindu rivers, the Ganges (called the Ganga by Indians), leaves the Himalaya Mountains for the plains of north India. The journey of over 230 kilometres had been a protracted affair, since there were many stops on the way. I got off at the bus station, which was surrounded by refreshment stalls; the air smelled of fruit, tea and fried snacks. Taxis and motorized rickshaws offered me their services. None of them, however, had a meter; the driver gave you a quick appraising look and named the price. This, I told myself, was perhaps because Hardwar – meaning 'the door of Hari'; Hari being another name for Vishnu the Preserver – is relatively small for a city that has been a centre of pilgrimage for the last thirteen centuries.

I got into a bicycle rickshaw. The powerful young man pedalling it smiled guilelessly.

'Why do you want to stay at the Tourist Bungalow?' he suddenly asked.

Yes, why indeed? Just because a friend who knew his way around had advised it to me. 'Tourist Bungalows are good rest houses run by the Government at important places throughout the country,' he had told me. 'They are clean and comfortably furnished. Being off season, you won't have any difficulty in finding accommodation.'

The rickshaw man recommended two local hotels. The Government rest house was, in his opinion, too expensive and no good at all. He even offered to drive me to his favourite hotels free of charge. I had a suspicion that he got a commission for each guest he brought them.

'I'll follow your recommendation if I don't get a room at the Tourist Bungalow,' I told him reassuringly.

We were crossing a bridge. The deep-green water of the Ganges glittered in the sun. Then we turned right, down a road that seemed recently built, with the Siwalik Range on one side. The area looked rather deserted. I noticed the spire at the top of Neel Parbat Hill. It was the Chandi Devi Temple, I learned. You had to climb 3 kilometres to reach it. And the mountain range was covered with forest.

'What wild animals are there in this vicinity?'

'Tigers,' replied the rickshaw driver. 'And elephants. Sometimes one of them wanders about just where we are at the moment, especially at night, since hardly anybody lives around the place. Pretty dangerous out here.'

Shortly afterwards we came to the Tourist Bungalow. It was, in spite of its name, a large double-storeyed building painted yellow, with a forecourt containing trees, bushes and flower-beds. In the hall I was met by the manager, tall, slim, full of high spirits. Yes, I could have a room. How long did I have to book it for?

He smiled at my question.

'If you stay for one day I'll be happy,' he said. 'And if you stay for two days or longer, I'll be happy too.'

He rang a bell. A young chap appeared and took me to a room on the ground floor. It had a double bed, a steel chair and a bare table. The two wire hangers in the wardrobe were bent out of shape. A big window in the right wall looked out on the mountain; another one in the left wall gave a view of the Ganges. Both windows had a framework of crossed bars on the outside – a protection against stray tigers and elephants? In the adjacent bathroom there was no hot water.

'It's because of the energy-saving drive,' the young man explained to me. 'Power isn't supplied to boilers.'

Less than an hour later I was in the city centre, walking along the busy Upper Street, which is lined with shops on both sides. I noticed that there were many signs announcing chemists and doctors. Suddenly I had to jump on to the pavement as a lorry thundered past, blackening the air with diesel fumes and spreading a cloud of dust on fruit and vegetables heaped on handcarts or on stalls. I held my breath, with a handkerchief pressed against my nose.

At a big crossroads, I wondered which direction to take. I wanted to go to Har-ki-Pairi, the sacred bathing place. A stone there is believed to bear the imprint of Vishnu's foot. Vishnu is the second member of the Hindu trinity, the other two being Brahma the Creator and Shiva the Destroyer. I proposed to attend the *arti* ceremony on the Ganges. Every day, just after sunset, a service of worship and prayer, performed with music and lights, takes place there.

I asked a jeweller the way. He was seated beside a showcase sparkling with gold and silver ornaments inset with precious stones. He wore a smart turban; his beard was white. A Sikh, I realized with some surprise. Sikhs are mainly concentrated in the North-Indian state of Punjab. Their religion, founded in the sixteenth century, has much in common with Hinduism, though it does not accept caste; it allows liquor and non-vegetarian food but no smoking. I talked to him in Punjabi. In the course of our chat I learned that he had been living in Hardwar since the country's partition in 1947. How did he like it here? Well, he replied, one got used to things. I asked how successful prohibition in the holy city was.

He grinned:

'Hardwar is a prohibited area not only for alcohol but also for meat. And yet merely 3 miles away' – he named a place – 'you can drink any amount of whisky and eat as much meat as you want – of course at black-market prices.'

I had scarcely gone a hundred paces further when I was suddenly brought up by a large sign over a shop on the other side of the street. It said in English:

OPEN 24 HOURS

B. C. HASARAM & SONS (MEDICAL SERVICE)

CHEMISTS & DRUGGISTS

(HOUSE OF NATURAL HERBS AND PURE HERBAL MEDICINES)

INTENDING EXPORTERS

Suddenly someone called to me. I turned to face a bookstall to my right. The man inside told me that Shri (Hindi for 'Mr') Hasaram wanted something from me.

'Why, whatever can he want?' I asked.

'Just go over and ask him. Look, he is waving to you from his shop counter.'

I crossed the street and went up the three steps into the chemist's. A big fat man at the counter half rose and shook hands with me, introducing himself as Hasaram. With an exaggerated smile, he then inquired if I was from the police or the income tax office. I asked what had given him such an idea. He said he had seen me write something about his firm in my notebook. I had only copied down the text of his signboard, amused by the words *Intending Exporters*. So I assured him that I was neither a policeman nor an income tax official. He remarked that he was not worried and had nothing to hide.

'My business is honest and above-board. What can I do for you?'

I asked him about his plans as a future exporter. In reply he wanted to know where I came from. I named a city in Punjab. He was not in the least impressed. Then I mentioned that I mostly lived in Europe. This seemed to arouse his enthusiasm.

He began by saying that the Ganges had been receiving the ashes and bones of Hindus for thousands of years, and to die in it was for many people to attain salvation. Often the corpses of animals also floated around in it. Besides, the amount of sewage escaping into it at countless points must run into millions of gallons. Yet the Ganges remained the purest of streams. That was because its water was unique. It promptly killed off any bacteria that found their way into it.

'Have you ever heard of Soron?' he asked.

'No,' I said. 'Is it perhaps the name of a famous local bandit?'

He smiled understandingly.

'It's a place in this state. There's an artificial pool of Ganges water there. If you leave the bones of a dead person in it, they will dissolve in twenty-five to eighty-five hours at the most.'

'Quick work, I must say.'

'Yes, the Ganges water is really something special,' he declared, ignoring my flippant remark. 'Pilgrims bathe in it – here in Hardwar about half a million of them had a dip on the day of the last Kumbh festival. It's used for all purposes: washing, drinking and cooking. And the pilgrims always take some home. The water stays fresh for years in a sealed container.'

'How is that possible?' I asked.

He referred to the origin of the Ganges. In the religion and mythology of the Hindus, the Ganges is a goddess, known as Ganga, daughter of the god Himavan or Himalaya. She was a holy river circling the city of Brahma on the top of Mount Meru. A sage called Bhagiratha begged Brahma to send her to the earth to save King Sagara's sixty thousand sons who had been burnt to ashes. Reluctant to leave her heavenly home, Ganga rushed tempestuously downwards. She might have engulfed the world but for Shiva, who broke her fall on Mount Kailash by catching her and letting her issue gently from his hair – that is how the Ganges is generally represented in Indian art. The contact with her sacred waters freed the souls of the good king's sons from the ashes of their bodies.

'For that reason,' Hasaram concluded, 'some drops of Ganges water from Hardwar, Varanasi (Benares) or Prayag (Allahabad) – the three places we regard as the holiest – must pass the lips of a dying Hindu if he is to enter heaven. And a house in which Ganges water is kept is held to be a sacred spot.'

'So your idea is . . .?'

'To export Ganges water to Europe and America – there are millions of Hindus and converts to Hinduism there.'

It struck me that even the air from Berlin, London and Dublin was being sold in tins these days. I told him about this, remarking that his business had quite a future.

'Indeed!' he cried as if electrified, wanting to have my address at once. 'I'll give you 50 per cent commission on any sales you make in Europe. And you may rest assured that . . .'

Then I was walking along the street again. The sun had gone down. Soon I heard the distant ringing of cymbals and bells, with an occasional trumpet-like sound of a conch. So the *arti*, or prayer, was already in progress. However, by the time I got to the Har-ki-Pairi area, the service was nearly over. I looked down the ghat – the long flight of steps leading to the most sacred part of the river, with the Lakshmi Narayan Temple in mid-stream.

On the dark-green water sailed tiny, round leaf-boats with flowers and lights on them, launched by pilgrims.

I thought back some twenty years to a summer evening when I had last been there. I had arrived with my father's ashes in a jute sack. In no time I had found the man I wanted – one of the local priests, called *pandas*, whose job includes keeping the family records of various castes. Taking me to his cell-like room nearby, he opened a fat oblong book with a red cover. It contained details of the occasions during the last three hundred years when my ancestors had come to this spot with the ashes of their relatives. The last entry was in my father's hand. I added a few lines and my signature to it.

As the priest solemnly cast the ashes onto the water, I felt suddenly that I was standing at the meeting-point of all generations – past, present and future. I was only a link between the living and the dead, since someone coming after me would later do for me what I had just done. The mighty crystal-clear river inspired in me reverence and a kind of dread, as well as appearing to have sublime beauty. Afterwards I had walked for a while along the bank under a star-studded sky, watching the many lights in the leaf-boats float down the river.

Now too I watched them. But the soft, peaceful mood of that earlier day did not come back. A sort of commercialism seemed to have invaded the scene. I went down the flight of steps on bare feet, crossing the bridge to the temple. A loudspeaker was shrilling out a hymn. The whole area was lit up sharply by neon. Some worshippers still stood around with their hands in an attitude of prayer. The images of gods and goddesses there did not fill me with awe or with exaltation. I felt I was looking at them as works of art rather than as religious symbols.

On the way back to the Tourist Bungalow, I lost my bearings in

badly illuminated streets. The bicycles – often with two people on each – had no lights. Several times I nearly crashed into them. It was rather late when I eventually reached my room. Changing into my pyjamas, I put on a heavy woollen sweater. I looked at the Ganges outside my room, then went out on the veranda and down the few steps to the broad, paved bank of the river.

A row of spaced-out lamp-posts laid bluish stripes of light across the fast-moving stream. There was nobody around. As a child I had come with my parents on several pilgrimages to Hardwar. The memory of those days held, above all else, three images for me: the moss-coloured water of the Ganges; the green mountains; and two kinds of monkeys – the blond red-faced rhesus and the black long-tailed langur.

I stood there, lost in thought, until I felt cold. The rush and roar of the river struck a vague fear in me. A cold wind had got up. It blew all night through one of my room's windows that did not quite shut. I wrapped both of the blankets and even the bedspread tightly round me; but that did not help much. I woke up frozen stiff in the morning. To get warm I took a cold shower and gave myself a vigorous rub with the towel. For breakfast I had a couple of oranges, an apple and a banana. I finished up with a king-sized drink of whisky from the flask I had smuggled in from Delhi as a precaution.

There was a knock at the door. I put the flask quickly out of sight. In

came a waiter with the tea I had ordered the evening before. He was
slim and handsome, about 25, with a face suggestive of an alert mind.
Asked, he replied that he had been with the Tourist Bungalow for two
years. No, he was not a local man; he named his hometown about 100
kilometres away.

'How often do you go to Har-ki-Pairi?' I asked.

'I've been to see it just once,' he replied.

I made an exclamation of disbelief.

'I bathe out there,' he said, indicating the Ganges flowing past the
Tourist Bungalow.

'People come from all over India simply for a dip at Har-ki-Pairi. You
aren't an atheist, are you?'

'No, I'm a practising Hindu,' he said. 'But Ganga-ji (the holy Ganges)
should be in one's heart. I attach no importance to ritualism.'

In glorious sunshine, I went to Har-ki-Pairi to see what the sacred
spot looked like in daylight. The water was still cold so early in the
morning with just a few people bathing. For a while I stood above the
flight of steps running down to the water's edge. To my left an
excavator and pneumatic drills were digging through part of a hill to
make room for a building. Dust whirled about. On the far side of the
road behind me rose the grey shape of a rocky mountain. The noise
from passing lorries, buses and cars got worse.

I went a few steps down the road to a small bridge that took me to a
narrow artificial island separating the sacred bathing area from the
rest of the river. From there I had a splendid view of the temples and
the steps leading up from the water to the street level. I reached for my
camera. But then I remembered that photography was not approved of
here. All the same I decided to chance it. A policeman, carrying a short
stick under his arm, stopped by me.

'If one of the priests sees you taking pictures,' he told me, 'he will
smash your camera.'

Just after he had gone, a young man came up.

'In the time you've spent waiting,' he said pleasantly, 'you could have
used up a whole film.'

'But the policeman just said . . .'

'Never mind that. I'll stand guard for you.'

And so my camera clicked away.

I went back to the bridge, from where I saw the hills in the distance,
the boats and the other bridges spanning the river. I became aware
that someone was greeting me. Beside me stood a *panda*, a stocky man
in his mid-thirties. He asked my caste. I said I didn't remember, having
dropped it long ago. He asserted that he was not one to beg or pull
tricks, but an earnest man who believed in inspiring people with piety.

And caste, he added, was what you were born into. It could not be changed or given up in your present life. Where did I come from?

I told him.

'But you live abroad now,' he declared, indeed filling me with wonder at the correctness of his intuition, especially as he could not have noticed anything unusual either in my clothes or in my way of speaking.

Meanwhile, three other priests had come on the scene. I offered each of the four a cigarette. Half-naked men and women were huddled together for warmth in a corner of the island below the bridge.

I pointed to the group. 'When do you think we'll be rid of poverty?'

'Never,' replied the first priest.

'Poverty will end when the world ends,' remarked one of his colleagues.

'That's too pessimistic for me,' I said. 'You are men of religion. Religion ought to hold out some hope, some comfort.'

'There's no room for hope here,' said the first priest. 'The biggest cause is over-population.'

He then used a couple of ribald expressions. Coming from a priest, they sounded downright peculiar.

I asked him how the problem of over-population could be solved.

'If a half-hour-long earthquake were to wipe out two hundred million people, then maybe things could be put right,' he replied.

'And isn't there a less drastic remedy?'

He shook his head.

'People are steeped in corruption and dishonesty. You know what Akbar wrote?' he said, referring to the great Mogul emperor who ruled from 1556 to 1605. 'Akbar wrote with his dying pen that he couldn't have conquered India for yet another hundred years if the Hindus had been less self-seeking. Everywhere you have to hand out bribes; everywhere you see man's indifference to man. Our general misery will only go away when we have one or, at the most, two leaders to run the country; the rest of them should be shot . . .'

Taking leave of the priests, I reflected that it was the day of Vasant Panchami, the spring festival held mainly in North India. It seemed auspicious to visit Rishikesh, another place of pilgrimage, 24 kilometres away. I caught a taxi with four other passengers. After a while we were stopped at a check-point. It was an uneasy moment, as I still had some whisky left in my flask. A police officer put his head in at the window. He shot a suspicious glance at each of us; his hawk's nose kept sniffing the air inside. Next, the boot of the taxi was searched. Then we were cleared. One of my fellow passengers had a little girl on his knees.

'You get into trouble even if you happen to have a small bottle of home-made whisky on yourself,' he remarked. 'If prohibition is lifted here, as it has been in some other states, people can buy better stuff rather than burn their lungs with the rot-gut that sells at a murderous price.'

Surrounded on three sides by the Himalaya range, the road climbed through some of the loveliest scenery. Thanks to the festival, multico-loured paper kites sailed in the sky, and crowds of people went about in holiday dress. After lunch in Rishikesh I took a *tonga*, a two-wheeled carriage pulled by a horse. The driver was a loose-limbed teenager in country clothes. The horse, rather old and phlegmatic, had a white coat spotted with grey. From time to time the boy would strike it lazily with his whip; the horse would break into a gallop for a couple of seconds, then resume its slow motion. So the 3 kilometres took us twenty minutes. As I was stepping off the *tonga* at the ferry, a man in a cream-coloured suit strode up to me. Slightly below medium height, he had a neat figure and grey-flecked temples.

'Want a guide, sir?' he asked in an amiable, business-like manner.

'No, thanks,' I said.

He exchanged a quick glance with the *tonga* driver, who urged me right away:

'Don't miss this chance, sir. He's tops, the best guide hereabouts.'

Ignoring the recommendation, I strolled over to a low stone wall, beyond which the Ganges rolled on. The guide followed at my heels.

'You won't regret engaging me,' he assured me. 'The temples and places of historical interest on the other bank will remain a puzzle to you unless they are properly explained. You will find me a walking encyclopaedia.'

I handed him a cigarette; he struck a match and gave me a light. Then he named his fee. In his brown eyes and oval face there was an earnest look that somehow aroused my sympathy. I offered him half the amount he wanted.

'I am a man of principle,' he said with dignity. 'I never take less.'

'Actually I don't need a guide at all,' I told him, and it was the truth.

'I'm 45,' he argued, 'and have a wife and three children to support. And then I have my expenses too – cigarettes, coffee and the like. As the bread-winner I have to keep up my strength, you know.'

'Quite so. Lots of luck and goodbye!' I started down a path towards the landing-stage.

'Won't you pay at least this much?' he called after me, reducing his fee by one-third.

I did not have the heart to look back and went on. The ferry-boat was already quite full. A whistle blew, the motor chugged, we set off. On the other bank, I walked up the main street. It was flanked with shops, restaurants, temples and hospices.

I saw sculptures and frescoes depicting people and scenes from Hindu mythology. Then I consulted the town plan and headed for Lakshman Jhula, a place with sacred associations. Lord Rama's brother Lakshman – whose deeds are told in the *Ramayana*, the great epic of Hinduism, composed in the fifth century BC – is said to have spent his last days doing penance there. To my left the Ganges still shimmered, but then it vanished from view.

The path began to wind through dense woods. Placed all along it at short intervals were benches of red sandstone for pilgrims to rest. From a slope flashed a white house with figures in saffron robes on the veranda. It was one of the many yoga centres in that area. Occasionally I passed a thatched cottage occupied by a hermit. The tops of hills kept appearing and disappearing. Suddenly an advertisement for soft drinks caught my eye. Houses and shops, bathed in the glow of the evening sun, came into sight. I was in Lakshman Jhula.

I wanted above all else to see the Lakshman Jhula Temple. In the columned hall there was a pleasant smell of incense. A slim dark young man greeted me. The Brahman's sacred thread hung from his shoulder across his bare chest; the cotton dhoti round the lower part of his body was of a dazzling white. The young priest led me to a small circular building. It contained a life-size marble image of Lakshman in the lotus position prescribed for meditation.

'Lakshman practised austerities at this very spot,' the priest told me. 'But he looks very plump and well fed,' I objected. 'Have you seen the images of Gautama Buddha? Buddha went through the ascetic phase too. His pictures and statues represent him to be as thin as a skeleton.'

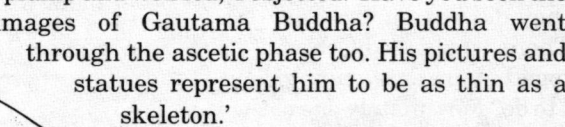

The priest frowned; then his forehead, painted with three horizontal lines of sandalwood paste, recovered its smooth look.

'Buddha was only a saint,' he said. 'Lakshman is a god.'

I also learned that this temple was an offshoot of the temple in Ayodhya, the birthplace of Lord Rama and one of the seven Hindu shrines.

'We offer free food to any sadhu (holy man) who comes here,' added the priest.

'Why do such a thing?' I asked.

'If you give in charity, the deed is recorded in heaven to your credit – you do it for your own next life.'

'But what about our present life?'

'God provides for every creature,' he replied. 'When a child is still in its mother's womb, the mother's breasts swell with milk. God provides even for those about to be born.'

'There was a famine in Bihar not long ago,' I said. 'Thousands died in it, including babies. How do you explain that?'

'It was their karma – the acts of their past lives – that brought about their deaths,' he replied simply.

To reach the famous Lakshman Jhula suspension bridge, I needed only a couple of minutes. Crossing it is supposed to be a mystical experience. So my mother had told me when I had left Delhi two days previously:

'Be sure to stand still when you get to the middle; the bridge will sway three times; and bliss is what you will feel then.'

Far below me, in its rocky and partly dry bed, the Ganges ran between the high steep hills covered with green. I looked down at the rapidly flowing water. Sunset seemed to lend it a coppery tint. Hearing a strange noise, I glanced to my right. Directly across the middle of the bridge sat five large monkeys that had not been there before. They formed a wall blocking my way.

I shouted something and made a gesture to scare them away. But they did not budge. They were staring at me with calm insolence. There was nobody else in sight. And I knew that monkeys when together are apt to turn vicious at the slightest provocation. What was I to do? Fortunately one of them suddenly jumped up on to the bridge's railing. As if in a trance, I hurried through the opening that had unexpectedly formed.

When I was at a safe distance I looked back: the railing was empty; the one monkey had rejoined its companions and sealed off the gap.

Later I told my mother how I had been cheated of the bliss of feeling the bridge sway three times.

'A bad lot, those monkeys,' she said. 'They were really mean – and selfish.'

Then she may have thought of Hanuman, the kindly monkey god, since she added:

'But one of them did, after all, let you through.'

Index

(Note: page numbers in italics refer to illustrations)